MAKING THE GRADE

A+ Advice for Parents

by Ginger E. Black, M.Ed.

A Lyle Stuart Book
Published by Carol Publishing Group

Copyright © 1989 by Ginger E. Black

A Lyle Stuart Book
Published by Carol Publishing Group

Editorial Offices
600 Madison Avenue
New York, NY 10022

Sales & Distribution Offices
120 Enterprise Avenue
Secaucus, NJ 07094

In Canada: Musson Book Company
A division of General Publishing Co. Limited
Don Mills, Ontario

Manufactured in the United States of America

Library of Congress Cataloging-in-Publication Data

Black, Ginger E.
      Making the grade: A+ advice for parents / by Ginger E. Black.
          p.   cm.
      Bibliography: p.
      Includes index.
      ISBN 0-8184-0501-5 : $8.95
          1. Learning, Psychology of. 2. Education--Parent participation.
      3. Home and school. 4. Academic achievement. I. Title.
      LB1060.B58   1989
      370.15'23--dc20   89-32520
                                                              CIP

MAKING THE GRADE

A+ Advice for Parents

For
ROBERT
with loving appreciation

ACKNOWLEDGMENTS

The inspiration that shaped this book began with the meaningful experiences of my own childhood. Those memories continue to steer me in positive directions as I relate to children today. I am, therefore, most grateful to my parents for their love, wisdom and guidance.

Heard throughout this book are a myriad of voices. Many are those of dedicated educators and concerned parents I have been privileged to know. The smallest but most powerful voices heard, however, are those of the hundreds of school children who have not only touched my heart but served as my most memorable teachers. I thank them all for enriching my life.

It is with warm appreciation that I thank my agent, Anita Diamant, whose enthusiasm and crusade never faltered. Similarly, I am grateful to my editor, Carole Stuart, of Lyle Stuart, for expressing an interest in educational issues and having the insight to recognize that we most successfully educate our children by best educating their parents.

Also, I am grateful for the assistance of the competent staffs at both The Professional Library of Montgomery County Public Schools in Rockville, Maryland, and the Perry-Castenadas Library of The University of Texas at Austin. They consistently demonstrated both patience and skill with my research requests.

Most personally, I wish to thank my daughter, Lauren, for the love she gave me throughout the life of this project. I will

Acknowledgments

forever recall (with a smile) how, even though she was very young, she displayed a mature respect and curiosity for my work as well as an unselfish independence during times when I felt certain she wished for a more available mom. Thank you, Bunkie.

And finally, words seem inadequate to properly recognize my loving husband, Robert. Without his encouragement and faith in me this book would never have been written. He appreciates it more than all others. It is, therefore, with unconditional love and heartfelt appreciation that I dedicate it to him.

GEB

Contents

Contents

Contents

Contents

MAKING THE GRADE

A+ Advice for Parents

CHAPTER 1

Making the Grade: An Overview of Successful Learning

Emily: Emily loved school—until the work became harder and the homework assignments longer. After getting off to a successful start, she now functioned more and more in a kind of "fog" at school and home. She honestly tried to do good work, but her "spacey" behavior really got in her way.

At school, she spent a lot of time just staring out the window. When her teacher brought her back into focus, Emily seemed shocked. "Maybe she just doesn't hear well; she certainly seems smart enough to handle the work," the teacher told Emily's mother candidly during one of their many conferences.

Emily couldn't seem to keep herself well organized either. She frequently lost things, and both her school desk and bedroom looked dreadful. Just last week she forgot to do several math homework assignments, and the science project she worked on for so long fell out of her backpack and never made it to school at all.

No one seemed more frustrated over these incidents than Emily, who was led to tears lately over almost anything. In the evenings, her worried mother sat quietly and thought to herself. "How can I help her? Should I tidy her room or organize her school papers? Maybe I should talk to the doctor and consider having her hearing tested. What would help make her happier and more successful in school? She used to be a bright, carefree girl. I feel so helpless—it's painful seeing her so miserable because of her schoolwork."

Emily is an example of a normal child experiencing school difficulty. She might even be labeled an "unsuccessful" student—one who is obviously bright, has no known learning problems, enjoys challenges, but is just not progressing well. Although she is currently showing signs of problems, they are not likely to persist throughout her school career and life.

As expected, Emily's mother is naturally concerned and needs practical help *now* to cope with Emily's problems and assist her in overcoming them. This book was written in response to the pleas that many concerned parents like Emily's have made for help.

The School Success Challenge

Why do we see so many talented, healthy children struggling to succeed in today's schools? Of course their parents want them to excel. But what more can they do after they've tried everything?

Questions related to helping children succeed in school are asked now more than ever before by both parents and educators. Teachers attempt to find answers to these questions by implementing educational research through curriculum changes. The solutions to children's difficulties in school, however, are often as complex as the problems they address.

The pressure our society seems to place on adults to "be successful" in order to be considered worthwhile filters down to our children, although in seemingly subtle ways. But such demands on children can become intense for many and unbearable for some. A child's reactions to the stress this produces—which often differs from adult reactions—can take any of several common forms: (1) emotional changes such as moodiness, disinterest or anger; (2) behavioral changes such as tantrums, fighting or disrespect for others; and (3) physical changes such as stomach or head aches, involvement with drugs and alcohol, and eating or sleeping disorders. Failure to succeed in school can be the consequence of one or more of these serious reactions to today's pressures on our children.

Parents and the home environment remain the greatest single influence on children. The school's influence, although important, is secondary. Consequently, most of this book speaks directly to parents and presents practical solutions for helping children succeed in school.

As an educator for the past 18 years, I have experienced the variety of challenges that occur when guiding children of different ages, backgrounds, abilities and interests. I have counseled their parents and teachers about their school-related problems. Through those experiences I found that, in spite of the diversity of problems that children have related to school, the solutions usually take the same few forms.

The "Making the Grade" Approach

The concept of "Making the Grade" is a comprehensive, but simple, approach to school success. Learning and good grades result from more than doing homework and succeeding with tests. As already noted (and detailed later in the book), a child's problems in school too frequently result from aspects of his or her life that are seemingly unrelated to school and thus not so easily detected.

Consequently, the "Making the Grade" approach concentrates on the "total" child—intellectual, social, emotional and behavioral—not just the obvious aspects that produce good grades. It considers the total child because all aspects need to be well balanced in order for a child to be successful.

To achieve this end requires a *team* commitment between parents and their children, parents and teachers, and teachers and children as students. By following a team approach to achieve a common goal, successful students—those who are "Making the Grade"—can result.

Organization of the Book

Part of the book describes specific warning signs common among children experiencing difficulty in school. By identifying problems early, appropriate solutions can be found more easily.

One chapter explains how children think and feel in relation to being successful in school. Parents who lack a basic understanding of children can become unnecessarily frustrated or worried, frequently complicating already serious problems. Therefore, greater knowledge of children in general can open many doors as well as tame specific fears.

Many parents who turn to the school for help with a child who is unsuccessful may not relate easily to their child's teachers or the school itself. Some parents do not understand schools and the way they work; others may lack respect or even fear them. Parents tend to perceive schools from their own experiences a generation or more ago. But the business of education has changed significantly in the last generation, just like other business operations in our modern world. Therefore, part of the book explains today's typical school environment. This provides a better understanding of the surroundings where our children spend most of their day and of the expectations schools and teachers place on them.

Another part of the book suggests how parents and teachers can work together more productively to arrive at practical solutions to a child's school-related problems. In addition, there is an entire chapter devoted to explaining the impact that stress and anxiety have on our children's ability to succeed in today's schools. Detailed explanations of how some of today's major controversies affecting school performance— e.g., childhood values, competitiveness and burnout—are also addressed.

To illustrate the points in many chapters, the book contains over 30 short case histories—like Emily's at the beginning of this chapter—about actual children and the variety of difficulties they encounter. Most of the case histories are drawn from my personal experiences with such children, although the names and certain identifying facts have been changed to preserve their anonymity.

Numerous helpful suggestions designed to guarantee school success are provided throughout the book. These include, for example, a fail-proof homework contract and even some exercises for parents to assess their own values and priorities that indirectly affect their children in school.

Finally, the book provides parents with many practical solutions for alleviating school problems and parental worry. These effective suggestions were developed by myself, other teachers and parents who have worked with struggling students firsthand. By using these methods, we have seen these children turn school difficulties around so they were "Making the Grade"!

CHAPTER 2

Warning Signs of the Unsuccessful Child

Children who are unsuccessful in school are unnecessary academic casualties. Most are complex individuals by nature and pose a frustration to everyone around them—parents, teachers and mostly themselves. They typically have from average to superior abilities, but for a variety of reasons find it difficult to succeed in school. Their fear of failure can be overwhelming and take several forms, often represented by behaviors that may not indicate their true potentials or backgrounds at all.

Just as no two adults react to an experience in the same way, no two children react to being unsuccessful in school in the same manner. Children are as different from each other in the ways they learn as in the ways they look, and each experiences frustration and fear of failure to different degrees.

Socially, unsuccessful children may appear unhappy with school or home, and feel negative about themselves or disinterested in the world in general. Sometimes they do not appear to derive pleasure from seemingly pleasurable activities. They may lack curiosity or the ability to laugh, and even prefer to be alone. Consider Billy, for example.

Billy: Billy, age 6, had near perfect nursery school and kinder-garten experiences. He was always cheerful and showed lead-ership qualities as well as a real zest for learning. First grade, too, started out well, but by November when the demands of school seemed more serious in nature, Billy began acting "bored" and lacked interest in most things at school and home. Even during play, Billy could end up in a fight with friends he had enjoyed for years.

Nothing appeared to be going quite right for Billy these days and he never seemed happy anymore. "Maybe it's a stage he's going through," his parents said during the difficult times. But maybe it was a warning sign of something more serious.

Behaviorally, unsuccessful children may be quiet, or "spacey," acting disconnected from the normal stream of things. Some show signs of gross disorganization and chaos in schoolwork and other activities. Some are unable to concen-trate; others appear not to hear well, while still others act depressed or moody—like Billy reacted. Generally, unsuccess-ful children are just as unique in their response to school failure as they are in the ways they react to anything else.

Understanding the Unsuccessful Child

All children exhibit some warning signs when they are experiencing difficulty in school. Parents, being sensitive and protective, are usually in the best position to recognize early symptoms and begin to correct a difficult situation to avoid even more complex problems later.

A child's lack of success gives both parents and teachers a sense of failure because each tries so hard to guide the child in the proper direction. It should be of some comfort to both, therefore, to realize that only about 20 percent of our children have some specific learning difficulty or disability. This statis-tic positively emphasizes that the other 80 percent—the ma-

24

jority of children—are capable learners. Consequently, most students who experience school difficulties do *not* have the serious permanent disabilities that parents and teachers so often fear.

Frequently, just a small change may be all that is necessary to assure school success for a child, or at least the beginning of a change for the better. For example, changing a seat in the classroom, turning off the television or rearranging a notebook may help achieve this goal.

At School

If your child appears to be having serious trouble in school, do not delay in getting support. Warning signs are cries for help. Delay only risks further complicating a problem because problems do not go away without appropriate solutions, but instead can take on a more grave complexion. By identifying a problem early, parents can help children overcome their school frustrations quickly while ensuring that their self-esteem remains in tact. Then all are winners.

When a student fails with a school task, often parents and teachers tend to believe that the student is not trying their hardest, which is usually not true. Most children try *very* hard to do their best job. It is their natural inclination to be productive and successful. They want to do well, be proud of themselves, and make others around them appreciate their efforts as well.

Too much disapproval or anxiety on the part of parents about a child's failure in school often encourages the child to give up—like Jon below. The real failure then comes when a child will no longer take the risk to try something new for fear of failing at it, a sign of a shaky self-esteem. This defeatist attitude can be avoided if the distressed child's warning signs are addressed early by parent, teacher and child collectively.

25

Jon: Jon enjoyed scientific challenges all his young life. He even dreamed of being a nuclear scientist when he grew up. Normally, he succeeded easily in school. But, this had been a hard year for him. He had trouble keeping up with the work load. The work had become so much harder and, to make matters worse, his caring parents showed great concern about the fact that his grades were steadily dropping, even in science. Each evening at the dinner table, Jon's grades had become the primary topic of discussion.

His science teacher, recognizing Jon's interest and ability, encouraged him to enter a project in the school's annual science fair. Jon listened quietly and then politely rejected the suggestion. He just couldn't face more scrutiny and risk another failure, and he didn't want to hear his parents' endless lectures about what a good student he could be.

Life was not pleasant for Jon. He had even entertained the idea lately of running away. After all, he was 13 now, almost grown up.

Outside of School

Most children try very hard to succeed, if for no other reason than because it makes them feel good about themselves. Sometimes, however, if the expectations placed on them at home or at school are too demanding, even the most successful child begins to break down, like Jon.

Adults can be quick to place labels on behavior they don't easily understand. Nevertheless, there usually are many factors that enter into a child's inability to put forth any additional effort. For example, many modern children live with unusually tight schedules of extracurricular activities. There is little time left over in the day just to play. Heavy demands with little relief can leave even successful children anxious and prevent them from focusing on important elements of their lives—schoolwork, for instance. As a result, this can lead to common problems such as "performance overload."

Warning Signs of the Unsuccessful Child

High levels of anxiety directly affect the way children concentrate on schoolwork. Like adults, children need to feel a sense of control over their lives; it helps them feel anchored. It is the parents' responsibility, therefore, to support and encourage a child's endeavors in positive ways as well as help them react appropriately when life becomes too anxiety-provoking. Paul was such a victim . . .

Paul: Paul had always been the pride of his family. He was a perfect baby, and the entire family marveled at how quickly he learned everything. He was even reading before he entered kindergarten! With just a little extra tutoring time spent with his devoted mother, he was able to qualify for gifted and talented classes in the third grade.

Since he was so bright and curious, his parents enrolled him in some stimulating computer classes after school. He enjoyed them a lot—almost as much as the school newspaper and student government. But his favorite activity by far was soccer. The team met three times a week before dinner to practice for the weekly Saturday morning games. This was a special time that Paul spent with Dad, who was always there on the line yelling encouraging suggestions of how to play better. On the surface, life seemed great.

Recently, however, Paul couldn't seem to remember things; mostly all those long-term homework assignments. They piled up unfinished on his desk and soon his grades began slipping. He had so much on his mind. Paul became frustrated and confused. Now, mid-year, his teachers were meeting to reassess whether Paul should even be in the gifted and talented classes. His mother and father were devastated when they learned of the teachers' concerns during a parent/teacher conference.

Children frequently react to being unsuccessful in some unpredictable ways. Like adults, children are unique and individualistic in the ways they attempt to cope during difficult

27

times. Teachers may be more aware than parents of the common warning signs children exhibit under stress. This is because they tend to see many more children and have learned through experience to recognize symptoms of frustration that sometimes lead to serious difficulties.

The accompanying table, "Common Warning Signs of Unsuccessful Children," is a compilation of the most common warning signs exhibited by children as they struggle to deal with the overwhelming and often frightening feelings of being unsuccessful in school. Each warning sign is discussed in detail in the remainder of this chapter and concludes with a brief prescription for beginning to correct some or all of the problem. These prescriptions are explained in greater detail in various parts of the subsequent chapters. There also is a comprehensive checklist located at the end of the chapter to help parents better assess their child's warning signs.

REVIEW OF THE COMMON WARNING SIGNS

Physical Symptoms

Eating disorders. Childhood eating disorders are very common (especially with adolescents) and may be a manifestation of stress. Such disorders can be indicative of underlying emotional difficulties, taking the form of physical disorders. Some children with eating disorders eat too much, some too little, while others may not want to eat anything at all. Some become rigid about the kinds of food they will eat, usually perseverating on the same few familiar choices. Unless diagnosed and controlled promptly, many of these children will require medical attention and counseling to help them once again feel in good control of their lives.

Fatigue. Fatigue does not automatically mean a child is tired. It can be a sign of poor nutrition or even anxiety in children. Trying to succeed with no resulting success is hard

28

Common Warning Signs of Unsuccessful Children

Physical Symptoms	Behavioral Symptoms	Emotional Symptoms
Eating Disorders	Boredom	Mood Changes
Fatigue	Poor Listening/	Preoccupation
Sleep Disorders	Memory Skills	Crying about
Nervous Habits	Disinterest in	Schoolwork
Physical Ailments	Learning	School-Related
Inadequate	Deficient	Fears
Nutrition	Organizational	
	Skills	
	Inadequate Study	
	Skills	
	Irresponsibility	
	Destructiveness	
	Extremes	
	Lethargy	
	Concealing	
	Schoolwork	

work and exhausting. Discouraged children often try to save face by portraying an image of success to those around them, often in exaggerated ways. Sometimes they vacillate between taking risks to succeed and avoiding the risks entirely. This inner turmoil can leave children emotionally drained and very tired, frequently resulting in daily mental as well as physical fatigue. Children subject to fatigue need adequate rest and plenty of time to relax and unwind at the end of every hectic day.

Sleep disorders. Radical changes in sleep patterns can indicate disturbance within a child. Changes may include sleeping too much, too little, increase in nightmares, sleepwalking, or sudden onset of enuresis (bed-wetting). Such sleep disorders may be an indication of emotional turmoil, which should be taken seriously. When such a situation occurs and persists, parents should obtain medical attention first, followed by counseling, if appropriate, to diagnose the origin of the disorder.

Nervous habits. Tics, thumb-sucking, stuttering, nail biting, excessive talking or unusual shyness, are all examples of nervous behaviors that frequently develop during a time when children feel anxious or unsuccessful. Directly pointing out negative behaviors to children (particularly during stressful times) rarely helps and often makes matters worse. Trying to teach children to break unpleasant habits when they are already stressed tends to discourage them further. Only a sensitive understanding of the source of the problem and removing the distressing situation will help to relieve such anxious children. Hopefully, it also will eliminate, or at least lessen, the bad habit in natural ways. Offensive habits usually will not disappear until the underlying problems are resolved.

Physical ailments. Some children react to distress by becoming phobic or fearful. As a reaction to worry, they can develop suffering physical ailments that prevent them from being healthy at school or home. These ailments can be triggered by emotional difficulties. Most common in school children are the complaints of headaches and stomachaches.

Typically, worried children become so overly concerned and upset internally about not being successful that they make themselves physically ill. Most of the time this is not a conscious act on the part of the child but a reaction to worry. It can serve them well, however, in that physical ailments can allow children to remove themselves from a stressful classroom situation, for example, and seek comfort and attention in a bathroom or sympathetic school nurse's office. Many make a phone call to a parent and eventually go home, removing them from a stressful situation entirely without resolving the problem. Therefore, the physical ailments usually return once again when the stress is reintroduced.

Parents should monitor and treat a child's physical complaints as real, for obvious reasons, being careful not to overreact to them, especially during times when you know the child is worried about school. Time should be spent not only to find solutions to the anxiety-producing situations that lead to the child's illness but also in seeking out activities that encourage anxious children to relax and escape worries.

Inadequate nutrition. Through research and casual observations, we know that proper nutrition enhances a child's ability to concentrate and perform well at school tasks. Nutrition is just as important as proper rest, exercise and relaxation. Children work markedly better when encouraged to eat a balanced breakfast, for instance.

Unfortunately, too many children do not eat a proper breakfast, usually because they are too rushed to get to school. Those who go to school without an adequate breakfast are often depleted of their energy by mid morning, typically at peak times for school performance. They become not only hungry but lethargic and unable to concentrate well. Because so much of a child's energy is used in growing, there seems to be little in reserve to rely on when their energy is depleted—

unlike adults, who are no longer growing and do not require such rigid eating schedules. Thus, adequate morning nutrition is essential and should not be overlooked.

Parents are more aware today of how food additives, artificial colors, pesticides, extra sugars, processing, etc., can have a negative effect on a child's behavior, resulting in attention deficit disorder, hyperactivity, and the like. An unsuccessful child's nutritional habits should be carefully reviewed and controlled by parents. It is one of the easiest habits to monitor and change positively to help a child be better equipped to succeed in school. Your child's doctor also can provide additional information on nutrition and recommend books on children's nutrition and specific related health problems.

Behavioral Symptoms

Boredom. Boredom is not a universal sign of brightness in children as so many adults believe. Bright children can usually find something to occupy their minds, even if it is mischievous! Boredom is more often a sign of withdrawal from problems or gross disorganization, caused by an inability to concentrate and focus on specific tasks. It also can be a reaction to anxiety. A child may seem "bored," for example, when overwhelmed with the fear of not being able to cope or succeed with challenging academic or social demands.

Parents should regard complaints of boredom with some degree of concern. Although unsuccessful children can act bored, it is nevertheless one of the less serious symptoms dealt with here. Most often, an honest discussion about interests, disinterests and fears can lead to some simple and satisfying changes for a child to feel better connected to the classroom environment as well as the home.

Poor listening/memory skills. Most school-related listening difficulties, contrary to what one might think, have little to

32

do with the physical act of hearing sounds. Nevertheless, a hearing test should be considered to rule out this possibility for any child who has difficulty with listening skills.

Poor listening and memory skills frequently go together. Children who have a difficult time focusing their energies on listening or remembering what they hear are frustrated themselves as well as frustrating to those around them. Often, they can be so preoccupied about their inner world that they are unable to concentrate on school tasks.

Some children, in contrast, merely develop a bad habit of not listening or remembering well, just as they would develop any other destructive habit. These children have learned somehow to regard listening or memory skills as unimportant, possibly because the skills tend to be more passive or intangible than active, and possibly because of the lack of importance placed on learning listening skills well during their early developmental years.

Poor listening skills may result in not being able to follow through with directions at school or home—or even remember what to do next—because of not "hearing" directions. In addition, these children may not easily remember such common things as:

- two or more step directions
- lunch money
- coats and personal possessions
- school supplies
- telephone messages
- overdue library books
- borrowed toys
- what to take to scouts, soccer, etc.
- who called on the telephone
- what to buy in a store
- what someone said.

The forgetting of these everyday events is a source of great frustration not only to children but also to their parents and teachers.

Parents can help children sharpen their listening skills by such simple changes as: (1) always using their name before saying something important to them, (2) providing them with experiences requiring multi-level directions such as in this three-step direction, "get the car keys, open the trunk, and get the things out that we bought at the store," and (3) consciously looking for activities and toys that require or encourage sharp listening skills. But don't expect instant success. Poor listeners are among those most reluctant to change bad habits.

Disinterest in learning. If a child is consistently disinterested in school, it is usually due to a specific cause. It is not typical for a child to be disinterested in learning or performing well in school. There are always other factors that interfere with a child's ability to want to succeed. Parents and teachers can help relieve such problems through open-minded discussions about the child's individual interests, complaints and needs. Teachers and parents can then follow up by working together to better orient the child towards the academic world. Teachers are receptive to encouraging children's interests if it would help them to become more comfortable with school. Teachers do not like to see any student fail; it truly disturbs them.

Deficient organizational skills. Unsuccessful students can suffer from gross disorganization. Their school desk may be unusually messy, and they may lack appropriate materials—not necessarily because they don't have them but because they can't find them. Similarly, they frequently forget where they put their homework, school bag or other possessions. Sometimes their lack of organization is so severe that it is difficult to focus on any specific problem or solution.

Disorganization tends to trip children up time and time again, and if left uncorrected, eventually cripples them academically. The resulting frustration can heighten their level of anxiety so that they feel miserable and may eventually be unable to perform at all.

Children must be taught that being organized and orderly helps to prevent or eliminate confusion, thereby promoting success in their endeavors. To this end, they must first see good examples of organizational success, most naturally through good daily routines in the home; then they can transfer those home-taught practical skills to the classroom.

Inadequate study skills. Many children who are unsuccessful in school are just considered lazy, when the real problem behind their poor performance is that they lack effective study skills. They do not have the necessary tools to succeed independently at school tasks. The lack of functional study skills holds them back.

This is a very real problem for many capable older students in particular. At more advanced levels the academic demands are higher, and without effective study skills to rely on students commonly face a great deal of frustration and failure. Many such students believe they lack ability in a subject when their lack of good study skills is the real problem. This worry takes its toll on the student's fragile self-esteem as well as their well-meaning efforts.

It is often not a student's fault, however, for these inadequate skills. Students do not necessarily know how to study, take notes, or organize information in an orderly sequence unless they are well taught. Schools should assume more responsibility for teaching functional study skills through the regular curriculum early in a child's schooling. Parents should expect schools to take on this challenge more vigorously. Through productive parent/teacher conferences, this need can be discussed so as to seek practical and tangible solutions, particularly regarding an unsuccessful student.

At home, parents should show children, by way of example, how polished study skills can help make life easier. Note-taking skills, for instance, can be transferred to (or from) the ability to make lists, organize time effectively, and maintain calendars. As adults know, fine-tuned study skills will serve a child throughout life.

Irresponsibility. Too many of today's children do not appear to regard the value of being responsible as an important value, possibly because it is not emphasized by parents in the home. Too frequently, children are not held accountable for family responsibilities, such as chores, and thus assume they should not be held accountable for school responsibilities either (e.g., timed assignments and homework).

Children need to experience responsibility early in life in order to learn the associated cause and effect. They should find success with their responsibilities, and see the positive consequences of acting in a responsible way. As a consequence, they will be better prepared to understand and handle responsibilities at school.

Not encouraging responsibilities in the home causes a serious disservice to a child. It confuses them because it produces a double standard of expectations—one for home, where little or no responsibility is expected or required, and one for school, where high levels of responsibility and independence are the norm. Understandably, this conflict can leave a child confused and insecure.

Skills valued as important at home should correlate with similar values at school. Candid discussions among family members can help establish some reasonable division of responsibilities at home for *all* members of the family, and in the long run help children cope with the demands of school in a more positive way.

Destructiveness. Some children, distressed over being unsuccessful in school, resort to uncharacteristic outbursts, sometimes with no apparent logic. They may abuse personal and public property, fight with other children, or even hurt themselves (accidentally or intentionally). Such children, obviously unhappy, feel a need to express anger and frustration at a world they sense may be betraying them. These powerful feelings should be dealt with quickly and firmly by parents before there are disastrous results. Counseling intervention, working with the child individually or the entire family, may be required to sort out what motivates such intense feelings and to help give the child some relief.

Extremes. Preoccupation with any excessive behavior may be a warning sign of a child who wishes to withdraw from what they may unconsciously perceive as unsafe and threatening— even school, for instance. Instead of confronting such uncomfortable feelings, many children turn to extreme behaviors to avoid dealing with what really upsets them. Parents should be aware, for example, of a child who rather suddenly wants to:

- read constantly
- watch television excessively
- eat continuously
- talk incessantly
- sleep all the time

Frank discussions about their behavior and what motivates it, as well as appropriate substitute activities, usually offer most children relief. Frequently, they just need to confront their fears and find appropriate solutions in order to feel part of a safe world again. This may require not only parental or professional counseling but also just time to allow these discussions to settle.

Lethargy. All children experience anxiety and worry about school at some time in their educational career; it is very normal. But some children appear more sensitive and unable to cope with it than others. Worried children are frightened children. They may choose to withdraw from typically enjoyable activities at school or home, act depressed and drained of energy, and prefer to quietly escape within themselves to feel

37

safe and in control. When adults are anxious they rationalize, "I'll get a headache if I don't slow down," or "My stomach will hurt if I don't relax." But children generally don't understand the link between physical ailments and anxiety. When these occur, therefore, they usually are unable to do anything about them because they are unable to focus on the cause of the anxiety.

Very often, however, by simply talking calmly in an accepting manner to anxious children and relating what you think they are feeling, many will discuss their emotions and, in time, begin to feel more optimistic about their life. If you are lucky enough to discover the exact problem, sometimes you can actually watch their fears and worries begin to fade away while you are talking.

Concealing schoolwork. Children who are reluctant to share their work with teachers or family are usually not proud of their endeavors. Many do not want to appear less than perfect to themselves or others, or admit they are having trouble in school. Students feel very vulnerable when they have to share their work.

Parents should not overreact to their children's reluctance to share work. Instead, they should gently encourage them to share selected portions of their work—parts they are proud of and feel comfortable about sharing. Such reluctant children usually possess a fragile self-esteem and are acutely sensitive to criticism in all forms, no matter how well-meaning and tactfully given.

Emotional Symptoms

Mood changes. Be sensitive to children whose personality appears to change abruptly. Such behaviors often indicate they are unhappy with their life. Typical negative changes in childhood behavior that are commonly observed at school include:

- excessive crying
- unusual irritability
- easily distractible and fidgety
- daydreaming at inappropriate times
- lack of spontaneous laughter and giggling
- emotionally detached or unreactive behavior
- sudden outbursts of aggression or hostility
- unprovoked tantrums
- extreme cravings for attention, usually at inappropriate times

These are just some of the signs of a child who appears to be overly moody. They should be discussed openly with the child in a patient and loving manner after an incident, not during, to help focus on the causes and determine some possible solutions. Because this or any of the other emotional symptoms discussed below may have causes that a parent cannot correct, medical or psychological counseling should be considered when appropriate.

Preoccupation. Vagueness and confusion are common traits of a preoccupied child. Because children are honest with their emotions, they tend to exhibit similar behaviors, both at home and at school. Therefore, if children appear preoccupied at school, they will most typically exhibit similar preoccupations at home. At school, such preoccupation may affect:

- general attentiveness in class
- understanding of assignment details
- meeting deadlines
- comprehension of what is being studied
- knowing where school materials are located
- concentration, even for enjoyable activities such as television or play
- ability to follow thoughts, conversations or directions

For teachers, a child's detached and preoccupied behavior raises a red flag of concern faster than most other behaviors. It is impossible to teach a child when he or she is not there! An effective parent/teacher conference can begin to focus on some underlying reasons the child might be preoccupied. By sharing information obtained from both the parent's and teacher's perspectives, they can take appropriate action to correct the child's problem(s).

Crying over schoolwork. It is always upsetting for parents and teachers to see children upset over schoolwork, especially when it produces tears. Children's crying should be taken seriously because they are usually "crying" for help.

Consider, for instance, what can result from homework assignments. Homework should be a review of skills already introduced and mastered sufficiently in the classroom for the child to practice *independently* at home, but homework frequently creates the most tears of all schoolwork frustrations. The *cause* for the tears is what is most important, however, and should probably be the focus of parental concern, not the actual assignments that provoked the tears. For example, a child may not have the study, organizational or other academic skills necessary to complete the homework successfully, thus becoming frustrated and reacting by crying.

Parents should intervene in homework *only* if the child asks that they do so. If children want parents to look over their work or help in some way, it is appropriate that they expect their parents will do so. However, it is not appropriate for parents to do homework with or for a child. Homework should be the independent responsibility of the child. Such "help," even with upset children, indirectly suggests that the child is incapable and helpless. It will also encourage the child to become dependent on the parent's involvement, including those times when there is no real need. Any overzealous involvement by a parent in a child's school work also serves to provide the child with a sense of control over a parent's time,

40

which unfortunately may end up in a negative and sometimes punitive way.

School-related fears. Many children, absorbed with the business of trying to succeed, lose sight of the pleasures of learning and become fearful about such school-related matters as making mistakes. For example, some children erase more than they write, or end up not writing anything at all for fear that it might be wrong or not good enough. If they do write, they frequently will not share it with anyone because they see little worth in it and fear the judgment of others.

Similarly, some children become overly nervous when expected to work in a timed situation, such as a math quiz or standardized test. Their emotional being appears fragile and their nerves seem close to the surface. Typically, they appear to be perfectionistic and hard task masters of themselves. Parents of such children need to react in only gently and supportive ways. These children need much encouragement of their efforts and little or no criticism of their achievements (or lack thereof). In this way, they will improve their confidence and self-esteem, as well as talk out what makes them most fearful.

In the end, the most positive support parents can provide for helping children succeed with any schoolwork is to be sure they that know it matters that they perform to their best ability. Some students don't feel motivated to do well in school because they think no one at home really cares.

A WORD ABOUT "EXCEPTIONAL" CHILDREN

Most children have good learning abilities, although sometimes it may be difficult to accurately assess them. As is well known, children grow physically and intellectually at different rates. These rates differ from time to time within a child as well as between children of the same age. Therefore, some lagging in specific areas is expected and very normal and, for most children, it does not suggest a serious difficulty, retardation or learning disability.

In educational jargon, "exceptional" children refers to those whose educational needs fall outside the regular expectations or mainstream of education. This includes students who are gifted/talented, learning disabled, emotionally impaired, etc.

A few children (only about 20 percent of the school population) have unique medical, emotional or learning deviations that are complex and impact on their school success. For this type of "exceptional" child, such concerns, including physical, emotional and specific learning difficulties, should be explored with qualified professionals—medical, psychological and educational. (The "Further Reading" list at the end of the book contains additional information about exceptional children.)

In addition, there are other students who are "exceptional" for entirely different reasons. They are not handicapped in any specific manner, but neither are they academically impressive. They may be labeled "late bloomers," "slow learners" or "underachievers," if labels help to better understand them. They perform adequately—perhaps even quite well—but at a slower pace, thus many have a difficult time keeping up with their more capable peers. To ensure that these students perform to their fullest potential, their unique abilities should be individually evaluated by their teachers.

Most educational settings have challenging programs for all types of learners. It is indeed fortuitous that we live at a time when schools provide vast resource and knowledge opportunities for children. Our schools are competent and eager to accept the challenges of meeting every kind of educational need.

STARTING ON THE ROAD TO SUCCESS

When working with an unsuccessful child in any area—behaviorally, socially or academically—it is always best to begin at a level where the child can experience some success and build on this for awhile before introducing new challenges to them. With this approach, children begin to feel safe in taking risks, as well as believing that the people around them are caring, helpful and, most importantly, respectful of their unique abilities.

Children who experience difficulty need continual support from family and teachers, often working together, in order to find success in school. It is time well spent because everyone knows that success breeds more success. The subsequent chapters of this book will guide you along this road.

Common Warning Signs of
an Unsuccessful Child

How many warning signs does your child exhibit? Check each that applies. Refer to specific chapter headings for more detailed explanations.

	Often	Sometimes	Rarely
Eating disorders	___	___	___
Fatigue	___	___	___
Sleep disorders	___	___	___
Nervous habits	___	___	___
Physical ailments	___	___	___
Inadequate nutrition	___	___	___
Boredom	___	___	___
Poor listening/memory skills	___	___	___
Disinterest in learning	___	___	___
Deficient organizational skills	___	___	___
Inadequate study skills	___	___	___
Irresponsibility	___	___	___
Destructiveness	___	___	___
Extremes	___	___	___
Lethargy	___	___	___
Concealing schoolwork	___	___	___
Mood changes	___	___	___
Preoccupation	___	___	___
Crying over schoolwork	___	___	___
School-related fears	___	___	___

CHAPTER 3

Understanding the Child's World

The Fragile Self Esteem

The most important and vulnerable part of children is their self-esteem. It influences their self-respect and self-confidence, as well as how they cope with our complicated world. A positive self-esteem allows children to "celebrate" themselves and their unique abilities, while giving them the courage and assurance to take those risks that are essential to become successful.

The positive ways children react to those earliest, successful experiences that offer them meaning—such as their mother's smile or the warm encouragement of others—help serve as a foundation for successfully handling other later experiences. Conversely, early unsuccessful experiences affect how they will manage new challenges as well. Negative experiences prevent children from taking the risks necessary to succeed in anything, especially school.

Since people have always been influenced by their surroundings, it is certain that children are no exception. Studies have proven that even newborn babies are so sensitive to their environment that they can actually recognize their own mother's voice among other sounds immediately after birth, because her voice was a big part of their environment even before birth. Most of us do not perceive of infants as being so aware and knowledgeable. The potential for their success at learning, therefore, begins at least at birth, or maybe even before.

Success at anything strengthens children's self-esteem and helps them better understand their individual strengths and weaknesses. Children of any age who do not have a strong self-image usually lack the confidence that encourages them to accept new challenges and become successful. As a result, their fear of failure may overwhelm them and result in "unsuccessful" endeavors, even when they could be successful. All children need to feel a positive sense of self-worth early in life so that they can then feel assured that those same confident feelings will carry them through even the most difficult and challenging of situations as they grow older.

Unfortunately, too often children's self-esteem is strongly tied to their achievement of goals—although they are entirely separate issues. Older children, for instance, frequently feel their academic and athletic accomplishments influence how their parents and peers relate to them. If they do well in school, they feel they receive both extra positive attention and greater material rewards. Similarly, young children also quickly learn which values seem to take priority and get the most recognition from home and school.

The most successful parents usually are the most sensitive ones as well, because they are aware of the differences between accepting children for themselves (including their individual natures) and accepting them for their notable accomplishments.

David: David was a large baby and now an attractively large boy. He was the first born and his family expected great things from him.

Fortunately, David was quick to learn—reading at an early age, sailing through difficult math problems, and now beginning his first year on the high school football team. Everyone was very proud of him but he took for granted the special attention his accomplishments generated.

In spite of all that was positive, deep inside, David really didn't feel that special. He lacked a sense of personal identity or a genuine interest in anything special. He was always "David the good reader," "David the math whiz," and now, "David the football star."

As a direct result of pressure to succeed, David had recently found fascination with a new group of school friends who were totally different from any of his longtime friends. They took pride in opposing values that David's family had always revered. They placed no great importance on his performance or achievement of goals. He was under no pressure to be "someone special" when he was around them. They seemed to like him for himself—just David—and he liked that a lot. He felt lighter, happier and freer. He thought his new friends were terrific.

So dressed in his new, unusual way with big plans for a different kind of Friday night with new friends, David set out to become "special" in *his* own way.

The Work of Play

Many caring adults do not easily understand the intricate feelings and thoughts of children. Grown-ups may see them as leading frivolous lives by adult standards and yearn to trade places. Sometimes, too, children are perceived as miniature adults, when of course they are not. Nevertheless, all children have some very basic needs (separate from adults) that must be met for them to thrive. Play, for example, is one of the most important necessities for children of all ages.

Play is not a frivolous act to children; it is in some ways a child's "work." Through the act of play, children learn real life skills that successfully help carry them into different social and academic settings. Play allows children to explore their environment at their own pace and in their own individual way. They learn best to relate to the world by the experiences they have with it, and play helps provide those experiences.

Children who lack or are denied plenty of free playtime can be limited in their skills and tenuous in their emotional reactions to experiences because they feel uncomfortable with the larger world. Children constantly try to understand and make sense of the world they live in; as parents, we recognize this as "curiosity." All children are born creative and curious. Playtime encourages both in a natural setting.

Today's children need lots of playtime; it serves to help reduce their level of anxiety and allows them freedom to learn in a variety of ways. Playtime should include time for hobbies as well as plenty of time for just relaxing—time to let down, rejuvenate and rebuild in preparation for the upcoming challenges of more new academic and social situations.

Many of today's parents, unfortunately, don't perceive play-time as the important time it is for children. They may regard playtime as "wasted time," or as time that can be compromised when necessary. Thus, they may over-structure their children's free time or deny them the freedom to play altogether. Adults, themselves, often lack enough free time to let down and rejuvenate, and on a superficial level may seem to cope with the over-structure in their own lives. They can therefore become insensitive to the value of structured playtime for their children.

As an example, children can be seen being carpooled after school to highly structured activities such as tennis, soccer, piano, science, art, ballet and computer classes. These children are not expected to participate in just one activity, but excel in several. Ironically, many of these "extracurricular" classes prove more demanding on children than even the regular demands of school!

Sadly, too, children are expected to appreciate, enjoy and succeed with these "extra" challenges, usually after a long school day when they are already tired. Surprisingly few children complain, however, probably because feeling tired is something children rarely understand until they are mature. Perhaps of equal importance is the fact that children want very much to please their parents—at any cost, like Peter below.

> *Peter*: Peter, age 16, had always enjoyed good grades in school. Even when he was very young he knew his parents already had big plans for him after school. Everything he had learned or participated in was in preparation for a successful profession in medicine, just like his dad.
>
> Now that Peter was a teenager, he worked hard trying to ensure his admission to a top college for premed studies. Lately, however, he found that it was much harder getting those good grades while trying to juggle his after school commitments to varsity basketball and a job in a local pharmacy. Weekends just brought a different set of commitments— chuch and social functions. There was little extra time to relax.
>
> Too frequently, when he sat down to work on his homework, Peter ended up falling asleep and, consequently, many of his assignments had either fallen short or went unfinished.
>
> It was clear that Peter was overextended, but with such high aspirations what could he eliminate? He was not entirely comfortable talking to his parents about cutting back because he was afraid they would look at him as a failure. If something didn't change soon, however, they would know he was one for sure—report cards were being distributed next week.

In viewing a child's "playtime" through this perspective, it seems no surprise that there has been such emphasis recently on childhood stress (see Chapter 10). After all, how many adults feel enthusiastic about evenings of highly structured activities after the challenges of a long work day? Not many—for most of us it's just too much added stress.

Children's Reactions to Difficulty

Unsuccessful children generally act more emotionally sensitive than successful school children. Their strong reactions to strife can be indicative of the high degree of stress they feel resulting from their school problems. Thus, relating to unsuccessful children's sensitive feelings requires good understanding and plenty of old-fashioned patience. This is even more important when you understand that children are generally more like adults in the ways they *feel* about things, but less like adults in the ways they think about them.

Since parents tend to be the most important people in the child's world, they stand in the best position to make the biggest difference in helping their sensitive children overcome school difficulties. The family environment, with its known structure and consistency, can encourage unsuccessful children to step out with solid footing and trust an unfamiliar world. During difficult times, most unsuccessful children can feel discouraged and isolated. A solid home life, however, can make the positive difference in their learning attitude that will eventually allow them to be successful.

Communicating With Unsuccessful Children

Children who experience school difficulty usually feel a greater need to know that what they do in school is valuable. They therefore need to hear plenty of praise and encouragement about their *efforts*—not just their accomplishments. Any appropriate praise given to a child must be honest and heartfelt, however. It will help to reassure them that they are respectable and valuable, as well as help give them the confidence to try new challenges, even during discouraging times.

Worried children may be so overly sensitive that they try to withdraw from their environment. Demonstrations of special physical supports such as hugs, smiles, winks and tickles during especially difficult times help to reassure them that they are always accepted and loved unconditionally by their family, no matter how they are doing in school. After all, if parents do not see them as people of great worth and potential, it is predictable that children will not feel a strong sense of self-worth either.

Effective communication between unsuccessful children and caring parents demands more than just hugs and kisses, however. It requires a great deal of mutual respect and effective communication—talents that improve only when unsuccessful children and parents act in respectful, communicative ways toward each other and see repeated success from their efforts.

Communication skills with children can be improved in such simple ways as (1) becoming, most importantly, active listeners to each other, and (2) developing more effective talking skills. Active listening requires hearing what someone is saying without attaching thoughts or judgments to the person's character. Active talking requires that the person's voice (child or adult) be recognized in matters that affect them. Good communication skills give all children a good sense of control over their lives. Moreover, children who feel a good sense of control regarding issues that directly affect them usually look at most difficult situations as their own responsibility and attempt to turn them into successful experiences.

Coping With Difficulty at Home

Children gain great inner strength from loving parental support and encouragement during tough times. Respectful discussions, words of encouragement and lighter, safer conversations with discouraged children provide parental attention in positive ways. These methods also serve to keep communication lines open so as to prevent children from withdrawing or becoming too anxious. Honest discussions about school problems help to let discouraged children of any age feel they have a strong voice in handling their personal situation, which inwardly, in the long run, gives them a stronger feeling of self-worth and control.

The lists below contain some suggested ways to offer discouraged students verbal encouragement. Teachers, remember, rely heavily on verbal praise to keep students motivated. Unsuccessful children, especially, need regular reassurance from everyone around them to keep trying.

THE SPECIAL LANGUAGE OF ENCOURAGEMENT

Phrases that Demonstrate Acceptance

"I like the way you handled that."
"I'm glad you enjoy learning."
"I'm glad you're pleased with it."
"It looks like you enjoyed that."

Phrases that Show Confidence

"Knowing you, I'm sure you'll do fine."
"You're the kind who can make it."
"You'll make it."
"I have faith in you."
"That's a rough one, but I'm sure you'll work it out."

"You'll figure it out."
"I'm sure you'll be able to handle it."

Phrases that Focus on Contributions, Assets and Strengths:

"Thanks, that helped a lot."
"I appreciate what you did."
"Thanks, I really appreciate _____ because it makes my job much easier."
"I need your help on _____."
"Your talent is _____. Would you do that for the group?"
"Looks like you're really proud of that."

Words that Recognize Effort and Improvement:

"It looks like you really worked hard on that."
"It looks like you really thought that out."
"I see that you're moving along."
"Look at the progress you've made" (and tell how).
"You're improving . . ." (and tell how).
"You may not feel that you've reached your goal, but look how far you've come."

SOURCE: Don Dinkmeyer and Gary D. McKay. *Systematic Training for Effective Parenting*, American Guidance Service, 1976.

Teaching Children to Cope with Difficulty

One of the best legacies parents can pass onto their children is a positive attitude about coping with difficulty. Most school children do not have many unsuccessful experiences to help them know how to deal with minor setbacks. When faced with such challenges, even on a social or recreational level, many children feel tremendous frustration and ineptitude about handling such difficulties. In other words, they are like most of us when we experience frustration—respectable, intelligent individuals who are temporarily having some difficulty.

Alice: Life was near perfect for Alice until her parents gave her a two-wheel bike for her sixth birthday. Learning to ride it proved to be not only the greatest challenge she had ever faced but also the greatest frustration. She quickly became upset, angry and discouraged. Since she was unable to successfully handle such a challenge, she blamed her lack of success on her father, the one beside her gently encouraging each effort.

Finally, during the second upsetting evening of trying, Alice threw the bike down and burst into tears. "I hate this new bicycle," she screamed at her father as she kicked it. Feeling pretty guilty for introducing such an "obstacle" to his daughter, he stroked her hair and tried to calm her by telling her he understood her frustration. Learning something new can be very difficult in the beginning he told her, but Alice wasn't listening.

So, unable to watch his bright little girl learn to cope with being unsuccessful for a short time, he rescued her by promising to put the training wheels back on her new bike. Then, she could ride it the old way and be the fastest biker on the block once again.

Coping with difficulty helps children build self-confidence. The child who copes well (especially in adversity) and sees the positive value in it, feels in good control and draws from those inner resources when times are especially tough. In contrast, children, like Alice, who are overprotected or encouraged to only engage in "safe" activities feel overly inadequate when unable to quickly find appropriate solutions for minor difficulties or failures. As a result, such "successful" children can act very unhappy.

Parents can help by regularly allowing real problem-solving situations to be included in the life of a child of any age. Using their own friends' problems or dilemmas as exercises is one effective way to begin. "What would you do if that was you? Why?" are open-ended questions that encourage communication between the two of you while forcing the child to think in problem-solving ways on their own before they really need them.

Making the Least of Mistakes

Many children have exaggerated fears about making mistakes in schools. Somewhere along the way, they learned (often before entering school) that making mistakes was bad and a reflection on them personally.

Making mistakes is one of the most effective ways we learn, and making mistakes is an inevitability in everyone's life. All of us will make mistakes as long as we live. No parent or teacher is perfect, any more than any child. None of us should expect to be perfect either. The sooner each parent and child accepts this fact, the happier and freer each will be to positively cope with the everyday challenges they encounter, especially those from school.

Dealing with Negativism

Most parents have faith in their child's ability to do well in school. By believing in them, parents encourage their children to believe in themselves. Such faith gives children the necessary courage to put forth their best efforts even during unsuccessful times.

Parents have the ability to gently encourage a child like no one else can. It does not take long to turn an unsuccessful student into a successful one when the negative or unproductive aspects of their learning are restated in positive ways, particularly by parents. By analogy, the glass can be either half full or half empty, depending on how one views it.

The parent who dwells on the negative side of a child's learning or emphasizes perfectionism—usually out of frustration and disappointment—unconsciously reinforces negative feelings that the child most likely already has. Such negative attitudes may eventually create a cycle of negativity—children viewing themselves as worthless as a result of repeated negative reactions they get from others. They may continue to see themselves as incompetent (even in successful activities) if they believe they are only capable of acting incompetently.

Consequently, read about James and reflect how conveying only positive opinions to and about children can help encourage them in *all* endeavors.

James: James was the third and last child born in the family. Because he was the youngest in the family, and very endearing, everyone showered him with loving attention. Perhaps this over-attention had contributed to his disinterest in using appropriate language until well after his second birthday. His baby talk quickly won James the label of "baby," first by his family in playful ways and then by others. "Baby James" was so cute, the negative nickname eventually shortened to "B.J." and stuck.

From the beginning, he lived in the shadows of an over-achieving brother and a highly motivated sister. Both had found school a wonderful experience and both had been successful. Now B.J. was in first grade and not succeeding very well. However, it didn't seem to bother him much, because he apparently thought most of his problems could be solved by flashing the beguiling smile he succeeded with at home.

In a conference, his teacher discussed her concerns about B.J.'s limited language and its relevance to learning to read. Both parents were naturally surprised, especially after raising two very successful students. They were perplexed about what to do now and how much to realistically expect from B.J. What had gone so wrong? He had had so many more advantages than his siblings. Everyone had done as much as possible for little B.J.

Relating to children in any negative way can be devastating, especially to an unsuccessful child whose emotional stability is already shaky. Positive stroking and gentle encouragement are proven ways to relate well. If a parent is not used to relating to their child in this manner, it can take practice. Old parenting habits are not easily changed.

At first, some parents feel insincere about emphasizing only the positive side of the child when the negative or problem side seems so obvious. However, with perseverance and a little time, relating in positive ways becomes more natural.

Most importantly, remember the child's self-worth is at stake here. Carefully chosen words to express adverse conditions can prevent further anxiety and destruction of a child's self-esteem. All children need to feel success and the sense of approval of others to have the confidence to move forward with new challenges.

Children and Learning

Most children perform as well as they are able to in school. Generally speaking, children are eager learners, and they especially love to learn anything new. They thrive on the process of discovering something for the first time and seeing how new information becomes meaningful to their lives. This enables them to make better sense of the larger world around them.

The fulfillment and understanding that knowledge brings gives children immense pleasure. All children enjoy getting smarter and feeling more grown up. Thus, it is not in children's basic makeup to not care if they do well in school, even though those might be the exact feelings expressed by discouraged children in school.

57

Children can be as exceptionally individualistic in their learning styles as they are in their physical appearance. Each brings a unique personality, individual prior experiences, personal goals and expectations with them to each school experience. These factors help them better understand what is being taught in school and why.

School is the child's place of work. It is not the only place they learn, and for some it may not even be the best place. However, since by law they have to attend school for most of their childhood, children need to learn how to exist happily and successfully in that environment.

The skills taught in school are not designed to be failure-provoking, but stimulating and challenging instead. Therefore, all new learning should be explained to children in terms of its functionality so they can feel satisfaction and relevance in mastering skills that will direct and enhance their lives in specific ways. They should not feel that newly learned skills are irrelevant, boring, or a waste of time. Children tend to feel this way, however, when they do not see their learning taking a recognizable direction.

Understanding Individual Learning Styles

Students develop styles of learning that work best for them because they are comfortable with those styles. Some students learn best, for instance, when they take laborious notes to understand what a teacher says, while others only need to jot down key words to grasp the same concepts. Still others may learn best by just listening attentively to the teacher without writing anything.

Environmentally, some students seem most comfortable with loud noises surrounding them; others need almost total silence to comprehend new material. Similarly, some students flourish when given freedom to interact with fellow students in a group situation amidst a wave of physical activity, while others require the physical restraints of a study carrel or quiet library to limit the distractions and concentrate. Students themselves usually find the ways that make them most comfortable for naturally succeeding with learning. Consequently, teachers and parents may need to take their cues from them, because they usually know best about their personal learning styles.

In recent years, classrooms have changed dramatically from straight rows of inkwell desks bolted to the floor to open-space classrooms where few walls, furniture or people restrict the activities. In addition, modern classes regularly use high-tech equipment of all types to enhance the lessons taught.

Teachers use a variety of approaches today to attempt to meet children's individual learning needs. Fortunately, through the exploration of various learning methods, we have gained the knowledge that individual learning styles must be recognized and respected. Parents, too, must learn to respect the individual natures of their children in order to be in the most supportive position possible for encouraging their efforts—no matter how untraditional they may appear. Possibly the most effective way for parents to understand how their children learn best is to simply observe them "learning" in a natural place such as the home.

Pushing Children Through Developmental Learning Stages

Skills taught at various levels in school are carefully matched with the stages of childhood development based on solid research. Educational curriculum development takes into careful consideration the various stages of children's physical, emotional and intellectual development when designing and implementing programs that hold children accountable for specific skills.

Educators know (as should parents) that children are unable to successfully learn certain skills before they have approached specific stages in their development. For instance, it is impossible for babies to learn to talk before they have reached the level of their intellectual development that allows them to make sense of language. Neither can they walk before their muscles have developed sufficiently enough to allow them to stand up.

The same principle holds true for learning academic skills. Simply put, new learning cannot take place successfully if a child is not ready.

Many parents either don't understand these very basic concepts about children or underestimate their importance. The facts confirm this when one reviews the increasing number of children pushed into learning academic and social skills that they are not ready to handle successfully. Pushing children too fast leaves even the most enthusiastic of learners frustrated, and too many difficult experiences will convince children that they are unable to accomplish *any* tasks successfully. The sad result is that many children cease trying, some at very young ages.

Children learn most new skills through a building process, similar to the way a house is built. A foundation of love, security and enriching experiences must precede any further building (schooling) to insure a child's solid success once in school. If a shaky or shallow foundation is a child's base, new skills cannot be learned well. Piling on more skills and challenges before others have been learned thoroughly usually only weakens the "building" until it eventually collapses.

Many children outwardly appear to withstand the pressure of learning skills before they're ready because children can be resilient and flexible about most things. But sadly, many children are too emotionally or socially immature to accept all that challenges them. When their good attributes (happy, eager attitudes, for example) are abused, children "collapse" under the pressure of learning too much too soon and develop any of the previously mentioned warning signs (see Chapter 2). After years of early struggle, it is not so surprising that many children give up on learning as early as third grade—just a few short years into their educational careers.

The Value of Review

A lot of what is taught in school is meant to be a review for students, particularly at the beginning of any school year. Most educators agree that new skills must be repeated to children until they are mastered or become automatic. This ensures that any new sophisticated skills, when introduced, can be handled in a manageable way.

Children who are experiencing school difficulty frequently require as much as 75 percent review work and only about 25 percent new material when trying to succeed in school. Hopefully, they can experience a tremendous amount of success with school work they understand, thus building their confidence, while simultaneously succeeding with a relatively small amount of new material. Consider this approach to teaching anything new at home or at school when relating to an unsuccessful child, just like the teacher below did with Tim.

Tim: The discouraged second grade teacher flopped down in the chair in the teacher's lounge after school had ended one day. "I can't get Tim to learn his subtraction facts," she said to the special education instructor who sat nearby. "He's good with addition but it's frustrating to see him work so hard and get so little reward from subtraction. He gets so angry with himself," she sighed. "I gave him extra homework to try again tonight. Maybe his mother or father will sit down with him. I have only so much time to work with him individually."

The special education instructor knew Tim and she had helped his older brother a couple of years before. "I have 20 minutes of free time before lunch each day. Send him to my room if it's convenient for you. It's quiet there and maybe I can help ease his frustration."

The next morning, Tim arrived at the special classroom with a stack of subtraction flash cards, a pile of unfinished papers, and a frightened look. He sat down at a table near the back of the room. The teacher greeted him with a smile and placed his work in an empty file on the corner of her desk.

"Let's try something fun," she suggested. She took out Addition Bingo because she knew he'd be good at it, and the two of them played three games. Tim won twice. In 20 minutes, he was chatting and smiling and sad to see the special time end.

The next day he came back to the special classroom and peeked in the door with a crooked smile. He played one Addition Bingo game again and then asked if there were any other games to play.

"Yes," said the teacher. "I have Subtraction Lotto right here; want to try it?"

"Sure!" said Tim. "I know lots of subtraction facts!"

Fear of Failure

The process of learning anything new requires taking risks—risking exposing onself, risking embarrassment and, of course, risking failure. All of us have experienced these feelings on occasion, but unsuccessful children can experience them frequently and usually with great intensity. Consequently, they can be tense and stubbornly reluctant to try to learn anything new, even when it's fun. They usually need many opportunities to try out a new skill before being convinced that they really are capable learners.

Children who are struggling in school need to learn in an environment that allows them the freedom to make mistakes—a major factor in all learning and a major learning block for most unsuccessful children. Mistakes, therefore, should not be emphasized by red marking pens and laborious reteaching, because discouraged children have little patience with themselves and take most errors too personally. Pointing out mistakes to discouraged children requires great tact and sensitivity from adults. Most unsuccessful children are bright and perceptive and are quite capable of seeing through even the most well-meaning comments of encouragement when they are not projected in totally honest ways.

Unfortunately, it is not always enough to just de-emphasize the failure side of unsuccessful children's efforts; adults must be very careful about not overemphasizing those successful times they do have either. Patronizing comments of praise, no matter how well-intended, can emphasize to children how important success appears to be to everyone around them. Such comments may seem well-meaning on the surface, but can entrap children into learning for the primary purpose of gaining some recognition from others. Remember, all learning should be accomplished for its intrinsic value; only honest, personal communication serves children valuably. Consider the following comments of praise as examples.

Incorrect: I'm so proud of your good grade on that spelling test. I know your father will be, too!"

Correct: Don't you feel pleased with yourself for taking those few extra minutes to study your spelling words before dinner? It really paid off for you, didn't it?

or

You have really worked hard to earn that grade— I'm happy for you. How do you feel about it?

The Imperfections of Being Perfect

Today's children suffer from many, not so subtle pressures to be perfect. Parents who strive to be perfect themselves in their career, appearance and actions, quite naturally expect their children to be "chips off the old block." They don't just want but *expect* them to be in the top percentile of the class, part of the highest reading group, on the best sports team, the outstanding musician, or ace computer whiz. Such pressures have the potential for producing serious anxieties in children, and can prevent them from concentrating effectively on almost anything.

An inability to concentrate in school quite often implies a disturbance or interference. They may feel inadequate about themselves, or their ability to live up to the expectations of those around them. When children are worried about their ability to perform, they often react differently than adults. Typically, many demonstrate an inability to focus or concentrate on important learning tasks, thus producing even more overwhelming emotions related to anxiety—bewilderment, fear, confusion or frustration (see the Cycle of Anxiety diagram, page 190). A cycle of anxiety can emerge, cause unnecessary problems, and be difficult to alter.

There is a great fear among our children that they will be unable to measure up to the high expectations that parents, teachers and society have of them. It is a real fear that knows no ability, socio-economic or age boundaries.

Some children can be too immature emotionally or socially at specific times to excel in all that is demanded of them, while others can be asked to understand and master skills before they have any use for them. Such demands leave our children anxious.

Even modern children's literature has begun explaining such mature issues as death, sex, divorce, handicaps and AIDS to children at younger and younger ages each year. Although well-meaning and often successful, such realism about the world when children are too young can contribute to childhood anxiety and cause children to become fearful about a world they don't yet fully understand.

Finally, children worry. They worry a lot—about nuclear

war, drugs, sex, kidnapping, family divorce and their own school performance. They worry, too, that their parents are so preoccupied and overly committed to their own lives (professionally, socially, etc.) that they will not be available to help them, as children, if their performance falters. Without that safety net, children become overly anxious. After all, if parents do not have the ability to focus on their child's efforts and successes with a genuine interest, how can the child be expected to focus on them?

Feelings About School

Most children try very hard to do good work in school; for unsuccessful children it can be overwhelmingly exhausting. Their simple school work may appear frivolous or insignificant to adults who have succeeded with it and moved on to more challenging endeavors. However, when adults reflect on their own school experiences, most can vividly recall only those experiences that were great in some way—tremendously exciting, immensely frustrating, anxiety provoking, or very unusual in some way.

Consequently, parents should be the first to be empathetic to frustrated children's concerns about school. Frustrated children need calm and sensitive communication from their parents, especially if the child's feelings about school are mostly negative. If children are to learn to feel confident and motivated in school (both of which lead to success), they have to feel strong support backing their efforts, not just their accomplishments. Consider Julie.

Julie: Julie often arrived home in tears after her long day at school. She sat down at the kitchen table and tried to talk to her mother about all the terrible things that had occurred that day.

Some frustrations involved interactions with classmates,

65

but many were related to the difficulties she experienced in trying to complete her work independently in class. Julie just couldn't remember everything that she was expected to do. Since she had no adequate study system, she would quickly become confused and nervous; then she would panic, draw blank thoughts, and forget everything she knew—even simple skills. Each day she felt worse about herself and school.

"Don't worry so much, dear," her mother would console. "These problems are minor compared to those you'll face when you're as old as I am! I'll trade problems with you any day. Go out and play and forget your bad day. Tomorrow will be better. Now, let's see a big smile."

Julie jumped up from the table, ran outside and slammed the door behind her. "No one understands me at all," she told herself. "No one ever listens to me. I hate myself and I hate everyone else, too."

Although Julie's mother was loving and obviously concerned, she offered little real assistance for Julie's "cries for help." Honest discussion and brainstorming about how Julie might overcome her problems would have supported Julie more than denying the seriousness of Julie's concerns. Her problems have now progressed to the point that she may need more help than her mother can give her.

CHAPTER 4

How Your Home Influences School Success

The Link Between Home and School

All successful learning experiences for children begin at home. The home serves, in part, as a haven from our chaotic world. Family members gather to retreat and rejuvenate in the secure environment that only home offers. For most of us, the home and family serve as our anchor. We cope with challenges better when we have strong family structures as our base. Conversely, these same experiences tend to disturb us more if we feel our family foundation is not solid.

The importance of the family is therefore pivotal to our success, especially when we are young and in school. Young children learn to feel secure enough to risk expanding their world after experiencing positive home experiences, and that naturally includes school.

In school, children generally enjoy the new challenges that it offers. Those children who are allowed the time to mature in a natural way at home—for example, not pushed to learn new skills before they are ready—are usually better balanced, more sociable and better achieving students in school. Unsuccessful students, in contrast, do not feel comfortable with the challenges of school and very often view it as a frightening place. "Why does learning have to be so hard?" some say. "I don't see anything fun about school."

Laurie: Laurie was the youngest child in a family of four and the last to attend school. She was a sweet child to have around the house and everyone enjoyed pampering her.

Laurie listened attentively when her older sister talked about school. Each morning she watched her sister saunter off to school with great zeal, eager to see her friends and learn new things. Laurie dreamed of the day when she too could go to school like her sister. She had hardly been able to wait until she was old enough.

A year later, Laurie entered kindergarten, but by mid-year it was not proving to be the exciting experience for Laurie that school seemed to be for her older sister. In fact, Laurie found many of the challenges overwhelming and all of them frightening. As a result, she worried a lot, she didn't interact much with the other children, and she was reluctant to try anything new. She needed constant reassurance from the teacher or children to complete even the simplest of tasks.

One day after school, the teacher sat down with Laurie's mother to talk. The teacher explained the important link between good home experiences and school success. She suggested specific independent tasks for Laurie to accomplish successfully at home that would better prepare her for the objectives of the kindergarten program. She also suggested that Laurie's mother help Laurie talk more about her likes and dislikes related to school so that the teacher could make school more personally enjoyable for Laurie.

Laurie's mother left the conference confused. She tried to mentally sort out the teacher's suggestions. Independent tasks of a kindergartener? Asking young children their opinions of school? "Does this make sense? Isn't this what *pushing* kids is all about? After all, my Laurie's only five!"

The home (and family) can be the greatest influence on children's learning because it provides a three-dimensional experience of living for children, while school tends to be the only two dimensions at best. Early successes at home obviously help develop skills and traits of self-worth that will transfer to children's personal school success once there.

Teaching a child attributes for promoting school success requires order, flexibility, and some teaching in the home as well as in the school. The teaching of the "total child" cannot be left solely to the classroom teachers or the parents, as Laurie's teacher tried to explain. Children learn all day long— three-fourths of their day is spent at home. The emphasis for the responsibility of teaching the total child obviously needs to be a joint effort.

Most young children today attend nursery school prior to kindergarten and record numbers attend day care prior to nursery school. (Presently there are about 10 million children attending day care facilities in the U.S. alone.) For working parents, early school experiences offer the perfect answer to career demands and child care. Therefore, the interdependence between home and school has become stronger over the years in an attempt to meet all the needs of our children as well as their parents.

Families at Risk

In recent years, cultures worldwide have been in danger of losing their long-standing family traditions due to our rapidly changing world. Our own society has become more mobile in recent years, as just one example. People today do not necessarily live where they were born or grew up. Families move freely from one part of the country or world for different reasons than their ancestors. Therefore, less significance is placed on roots and stability.

Our world also is getting smaller and faster. We can telephone anywhere within seconds and witness worldwide news as it happens. We can fly around the globe in a day and are capable of preparing a meal almost instantly. These are certainly advantages of our modern world; however, at the same time, families can be strained and put at risk under these rushed circumstances. The traditional family is fragile and needs protection more than ever to survive such rapid technological and sociological change.

Families and Structure

Every child needs and deserves to grow up in a comfortable home environment that functions around values that encourage structure, order and consistency. When the home is orderly, family members are relaxed and stress free. When it is chaotic and disorderly, family members are not able to experience the best of times, either together or separately. Order, after all, gives us freedom.

Important home values are always reflected through children at school. The values families cherish, therefore, should not diverge too significantly from values highly regarded at school or they may cause confusion and relay mixed messages to children.

Children who learn to live with disorder at home, for instance, generally act disorderly at school as well. Eventually, many become victims of their own disorder and suffer unnecessarily in the classroom. A messy desk, for example, can prevent a child from locating his or her materials or completing work.

Successful students, on the other hand, usually feel comfortable moving from appropriate home values to those of the school because, although the activities may be very different, the basic expectations are similar. Routines in classrooms are carefully defined so as to provide a sense of order for students while allowing them some freedom. The homes of successful children usually function in similar ways as well.

Unsuccessful children who feel overwhelmed by disorder frequently feel a loss of control. Children can feel anxious with insecurity with too much confusion around them and naturally try to create their own sense of order out of chaos if given the chance. They typically react by becoming stubbornly inflexible as one way of dealing with their anxiety. Their frustrations can often take the form of what adults label as discipline problems in the classroom or at home.

Predictable structure in life helps people of all ages make sense of their complex world. Children of all ages feel most comfortable knowing what is expected of them as well as what to expect. Many unsuccessful children seem to have too little structure at home to rely on and to help them feel secure enough about the routines at school to be successful.

Structured routines give children a good feeling of security because they provide a sense of orderliness from which freedom can then grow. Children are not, after all, miniature adults, and they are usually not as flexible about adjusting to unpredictable situations as adults.

Fortunately, it is not difficult to correct inefficiencies in the home to help children feel more successful in school. Routines are naturally created from such everyday tasks and times as meals, baths, quiet and homework, play, relaxation and bedtime and can take shape rather easily with some adult awareness.

Rob: Rob was born into a family of intelligent, free-spirited people. Their priorities and interests did not lie in achieving great materialism, but more in living life to its fullest. The family traveled extensively and viewed their careers as vehicles for a more casual and eclectic lifestyle than most traditional families. Home was where they hung their hat and gathered over an interesting meal with stimulating conversation.

71

Rob, their only child, had been raised in this stimulating environment, toddling off on long trips and late night restaurants beginning as a baby. He had never known a specific bedtime, daily routines or much structure in his life. Those regimens only restricted spontaneous activity, his parents believed.

Rob was a great asset to his class when he began school because he had been exposed to so many unusual and enriching experiences. He had a fabulous vocabulary and everyone at school seemed to like him. But Rob did not like school very much.

School seemed like such a rigid and confining place for Rob that it made him uncomfortable. His teacher was always reminding him to tidy his desk, hang up his coat or finish his work on time. Rob wasn't used to such demands and it frustrated him. Lately, he had begun to act out those frustrations by fighting with classmates.

The teacher called Rob's mother in for a conference about his behavior problems and general unhappy attitude at school. Rob's mother sat shocked. "Rob has always been a happy child until recently. We have taken a lot of time to create a stress-free, happy home to encourage Rob's creativity. He is a very bright boy but steps to a different drummer," she said. "You obviously don't hear his rhythm!"

Responsibility—Who's to Credit?

Responsible children emerge from families who properly balance love and discipline. Responsibility cannot be imposed. It must naturally flourish from within. Responsibility is encouraged and directed by the good values demonstrated at home and then used naturally in school. All family members must understand their individual roles and responsibility and realize how his or her part keeps the family functioning cooperatively. Families, after all, are cooperative teams, working together for common purposes and sharing in common experiences.

When parents do not perform their job adequately where they work, the turmoil this produces carries over to the home. It can cause financial or emotional discomfort, and the negative effects are felt by the entire family.

Children need to learn early in life that they, too, are relied on for family responsibilities in the home as well as their "job" outside the home just like parents. The child's job outside the home is school. Their responsibilities there are not to earn money to help support the family, but to enjoy learning to the best of their ability, be proud of their endeavors and make their family proud.

Many unsuccessful children—already feeling inadequate—do not consider themselves as important people who are relied on by others. Parents and teachers can work together, in a joint conference with the child, if necessary, to explain the purpose of school and their responsibilities there. Children should be shown the correlation between not succeeding in school and the adverse effects it has on themselves and their family, e.g., turmoil and unhappiness—the same adverse negative effects experienced when parents do not do their job successfully. This concept is not only logical but makes sense to children of all ages. Taking the time to explain it also helps successful and unsuccessful children feel well-connected to the family and worthwhile.

Irresponsibility—Who's to Blame?

Unsuccessful children frequently appear extremely irresponsible to many adults. They may be labeled "unsuccessful" in school, when actually they may not have been taught well enough to value being responsible at home before attending school. In teaching children responsibility, think of teaching them to *respond* to their good *abilities*.

As a common example, a child who lives around excessive clutter learns that tidiness is not a value of high priority in the home. Consequently, he or she usually does not keep a tidy desk at school either, and often becomes upset over just trying to find materials in class. Unfortunately, this same child simultaneously learns (through frustration) that orderliness *is* a value of high priority in school. How confused he or she must feel! As a result, the child must then decide to either continue along as usual or adjust the value learned in the home in order to be successful in school. This can lead to inner conflict, confusion and anxiety—any of which can interfere with their functioning, even with good ability.

To conclude, teaching children responsibility *must* begin in the home early in a child's life, long before they are expected to succeed with independent responsibilities at school. Parents can help a child learn responsibility in any number of natural ways—relating to family members, participating in chores and seeing the way others act responsible toward him or her.

Family Time Together

Families, as mentioned earlier, are cooperative teams that share in common purposes and experiences to enhance their relationship. Families who, for instance, work together to plan vacations, purchase new things, or share in work feel well-connected and supported.

Children, like other family members, should feel a part of *all* family activities, including such potentially unpleasant ones as everyday chores. Chores can be productive activities that satisfy many objectives for guaranteeing school success. Children learn to work cooperatively as well as independently and see projects to their completion, all "functional skills" that serve children successfully in the classroom.

In past generations, the family meal was a pivotal part of every day. Not only was it traditional, especially at the end of each day, but it fostered cohesiveness among family members. Through contact and conversation, all members learned to understand and respect each other more. Many children today complain of having too little family time together. With two-career families more commonplace, it's no surprise that more and more families don't even have the time to eat a meal together once a day.

Today's typical family is somewhat different from past generations. Many members are off in scattered directions pursuing individual interests, often unaware of where other family members are or why they are engaged in *their* special activities. The home is run with perfect efficiency around fast foods and microwave ovens to allow for such demanding involvement. Sadly, such efficiency also can become the enemy of our children, because children don't thrive under tight schedules and precision efficiency. The result of over-involvement in activities can be little family time left over for play and frivolity between parent and child—both of which are vital to a good relationship.

For any unsuccessful child, quality relaxation time spent with a caring family is essential. Even watching TV together or doing chores side by side can reinforce a close bond and encourage a child to relax, thus enabling school fears and concerns to be expressed in natural conversation. A relaxed home environment helps all family members function better. Walks, talks, and even simple quiet time together encourage all family members to relax. Children truly enjoy sharing in such ordinary activities where the time is spent in unrushed ways.

Young children thoroughly enjoy any time they spend with their parents; even everyday shopping or visits to the public library can be treasured moments when one is very young. In tagging along, they learn something new from each experience as well as feel closely connected to someone they love, thereby fostering skills that enhance success in school.

Managing Competition

The concept of competition is an important one. Competition can be a positive force or a major stress factor in any child's life. It can motivate us to extend ourselves and our abilities or it can cripple us into thinking we are incapable. Over-competition is even more important as it relates to children. Over-competition produces few real winners and, unfortunately, too many losers. A child who has a natural athletic ability, for instance, should be able to succeed with the competition of sports without provoking anxiety. If not, the activity should be reevaluated. Sports, as with all extra-curricular activities, should be designed to encourage children to have fun and relax, thus reducing their anxiety, not heightening it.

Nathan: Nathan, a junior high student, had enjoyed all sports since he was very young. He had been good at soccer, swimming and now football. He planned every moment of his teenage life now around football practice and football games. Even during his relaxation time at home, there was plenty of football talk or games to watch.

In the past, Nathan had been a fair student in school, but now his academic grades didn't receive the attention his maneuvers on the football field did. His focus was on sports, not grades.

Now that he was older, Nathan found that the pressure to perform athletically also had increased. Between the exhausting practices and the pressure to do well during the games, Nathan had learned what it was like to feel nervous most of the time. This made it even more difficult to concentrate on the school work that also had become more demanding as he got older.

Consequently, Nathan was now in danger of being sidelined this term because of poor grades. He sat at the desk in his room and stared into space. How could he ever face sitting on the bench knowing that everyone would be sitting in the stands waiting for his next great play?

Parents can unconsciously be the biggest offenders of encouraging anxiety-provoking competition in seemingly innocent ways. Those who encourage competitive activities for children need to examine first why competition is so important before passing such powerful attitudes onto children. Sports, as well as other "extra" activities need to be kept in clear perspective, particularly for already unsuccessful children.

Class placement, grades and test scores have also become issues or criteria for measuring children's competitive performance—even as young as nursery school. Some parents have been known to pursue particular schools for their children even before they are born! What personal objectives can parents possibly have for an unborn child? Are they really concerned about their child's needs or their own? What attitudes will these unborn children learn to value about competition and ambition?

For children who are attempting to learn skills for the first time in their life, particularly when very young, pressure can be discouraging, especially when they have just begun to discover the joy of learning.

Families and Respect

Every family member, from parents to pets, must be respected. Adults who respect children (even unsuccessful ones) teach them to be respectful and, in turn, to expect respect from others. Many unsuccessful children frequently act disrespectfully to people around them (very often to those whom they love and trust most) because they lack a basic respect for themselves.

Disrespectful children must develop a positive self-image

first, usually through appropriate attention and understanding, in order to feel deserving of respect from others. When they feel good inside about themselves, most disrespectful children feel uncomfortable acting in disrespectful ways toward others.

Unsuccessful children often can act in disrespectful ways when they feel they are not respected. They can lack self respect and have powerful negative feelings about school. Many feel out of control because, in fact, they are out of control. Unsuccessful children frequently feel that decisions are made for them without their input and that expectations are put on them without much consideration of their ability to succeed.

If parents were to include children in the decisions that directly affect them, both in and out of school, such dangerous attitudes would be minimized. It is a simple matter of respecting the child.

Teaching Respect for Property

Children must be taught to appreciate and respect all forms of property. Such respect is a value like all others, which must be taught in the home long before beginning school. Many children regard most of their own property as minimally valuable and easily replaceable, and they too often disregard the property of others altogether, at home or at school.

As a direct result of such attitudes, our schools have to cope with escalating vandalism and theft. Incidents from theft to arson in schools are regular subjects when formulating school budget objectives. Millions of dollars are spent each year just to repair the destruction of vandalism, when that same money could be used to improve our schools in so many other ways. Plastic, for example, is used in some schools to replace and prevent future broken windows, and security sensor machines have been installed in schools for libraries and laboratories just to attempt to maintain adequate educational materials.

Students, overly concerned about the value of such things as their personal appearance, frequently disregard altogether other valuables such as materials connected with learning. Lost library books, school supplies or even assignments are not regarded with importance; after all, they can be easily replaced.

Family Communication

Communicating is the act between people of giving and receiving information. Although we readily recognize that good communication is essential to family members, many lack the effective skills that help keep them well connected and strong.

Families who suffer from difficult communication problems, especially with unsuccessful children, need help, such as family counseling or parent training workshops. (Inquire about such through your family doctor or school counselor.) They teach families positive and effective ways to relate. Families who have taken the time to pursue such resources have found the training valuable and believe their entire family is better for the knowledge and time devoted to learning good communication skills.

Presented below are: "How to Listen to Your Child" and "How to Get Your Child to Listen to You." They are examples of proven effective communication skills for parents to think about and use with their children. Some examples of inappropriate communication techniques are included in "Roadblocks to Communication," also below. All three have good suggestions for making differences in the feelings of children about themselves, their relationships with others and, ultimately, their school success.

79

How to Listen to Your Child

Listen to the language of behavior. Tears, a laugh, a sullen face, a slammed door have meaning just as do words.

Communicate appropriately. Let children realize that you accept their feelings, whatever they may be, and therefore they can verbally express them to you if they so choose.

Learn to respond reflectively. Let them know what you think they are feeling at a particular moment without placing a value judgment on their feelings.

Be less teachy. Do not get so caught up in the idea that you have to be "teaching" your child something all the time. In doing this, you may overlook the problem of the moment.

Realize the importance of listening. Listening can play an important part toward enhancing your child's feelings of self-esteem and self-confidence (listening can communicate any number of different but overlapping messages—such as "You're a worthwhile person" and "I respect your point of view."

Be an active listener. Make a conscious and obvious effort to understand and care about what your child is saying.

Accept early language imperfections. Language does not always follow rules. Children who are constantly corrected when speaking will have difficulty being spontaneous in sharing their experiences or feelings because they fear criticism.

Realize the importance of eye contact. Look at your children in the eye when talking to them and make eye contact when they speak to you.

Start listening early. Communication between parent and child is extremely difficult if the groundwork has not been laid early. What is "important" is a relative matter and any child's concern is important to him or her.

It is never too late. Good communication patterns do begin early—but better communication is always possible and is ongoing.

SOURCE: Don Dinkmeyer and Gary D. McKay, *Systematic Training for Effective Parenting*, American Guidance Service, 1976.

HOW TO GET YOUR CHILD TO LISTEN TO YOU

Answer youngsters' questions. Be as quick, as candid and as forthright as possible. You can communicate any number of messages and make children feel they are important and respected.

Be aware of the importance of timing. When your child asks a question, it is a sign that he or she is ready to listen and wants your opinion. Be careful to choose an appropriate time for discussing touchy subjects with your child.

Don't play perfect parent. It is always tempting to know all the answers. Sometimes we do know best. But sometimes we don't and we are well advised not to pretend that we know it all. Admitting that we don't know is one way of conveying that we are not perfect, that we are human, too.

Allow for disagreement. Sometimes parents worry that allowing children to disagree with them will undermine their respect. Actually, children feel more respect for parents when they feel free to express their side of things. Permitting youngsters to

81

disagree with us shows them that we're strong enough to be challenged (and big enough to back down if necessary).

Avoid using sarcasm or ridicule. Humiliating children is a quick and sometimes permanent way to get them not to listen. None of us want to talk or listen to other people if we feel they will cut us down.

Allow children to express their feelings. Let them know we can accept their "good" as well as "bad" feelings—and still think no less of them. Telling children that they should feel differently won't encourage them to listen to you.

Watch the use of labels. Your perceptions should change from month to month and year to year as your child grows and changes. Sometimes we say things in the presence of children which fix in their minds for better or worse (more often for worse) our conception of them. Children who have been judged or labeled find it difficult to listen for fear of being judged and labeled even more.

Understand adolescence for what it is. Perhaps the hardest thing that parents face during their youngsters' teen years is their child's refusal of adult help and discipline. Growing up is no simple task. The insecure side of the adolescent wants to feel safe and protected—the adventurous side wants to grow up and do new things. Relating (advice, praise, discipline) should be geared to a young adult, not a young child.

Don't give up. Getting your child to tune you in rather than out at times seems hopeless, but you can do it—and probably better than you are doing it now. If you want your children to listen to you, they must know for certain that you will be available to listen to them.

SOURCE: Don Dinkmeyer and Gary D. McKay, *Systematic Training for Effective Parenting*, American Guidance Service, 1976.

BLOCKADES TO EFFECTIVE COMMUNICATION

Ordering, commanding, directing. Example: "You stop complaining and get your work done."

Warning, threatening. Example: "You'd better get on the ball if you expect to make a good grade in this class."

Moralizing, preaching, giving "shoulds" and "oughts." Example: "You know it's your job to study when you come to school. You should leave your personal problems at home where they belong."

Advising, offering solutions or suggestions. Example: "The thing for you to do is to work out a better time schedule. Then you'll be able to get all your work done."

Judging, criticizing, disagreeing, blaming. Examples: "You're just plain lazy" or "You're a big procrastinator."

Name-calling, stereotyping, labeling. Example: "You're acting like a fourth-grader, not like someone almost ready for high school."

Interpreting, analyzing, diagnosing. Example: "You're just trying to get out of doing that assignment."

Praising, agreeing, giving positive evaluations. Example: "You're really a very competent young man. I'm sure you'll figure it out somehow."

Reassuring, sympathizing, consoling, supporting. Example: "You're not the only one who ever felt like this. I've felt that way about tough assignments, too. Besides, it won't seem hard when you get into it."

Questioning, probing, interrogating, cross-examining. Examples:
"Do you think the assignment was too hard?"
"How much time did you spent on it?"
"Why did you wait so long to ask for help?"
"How many hours did you put in on it?

Being sarcastic, humoring, diverting. Examples:
"Come on, let's talk about something more pleasant."
"Now isn't the time."
"Let's get back to our lesson."
"Seems like someone got up on the wrong side of the bed this morning."

SOURCE: Thomas Gordon, *Parent Effectiveness Training,* Peter Wyden, Inc., 1970.

CHAPTER 5

Parenting for School Success

In past generations, parents had few guidelines to help them raise children. Children were to be seen and not heard, and discipline implied only physical punishment. Typically, the teaching of children was left to the teacher, and parents generally didn't question them or their methods.

Parents today, however, are quite different. We recognize that there are better ways to raise children than in the past. We no longer have children for the purpose of passing on the family business or having help when we become old. Instead, parents are more thoughtful about having children and their ultimate fate. We celebrate how children make our lives more meaningful, but at the same time we are well aware that having them is a serious responsibility as well as a lifelong commitment.

Today's modern parents seek out information in any form related to helping us successfully parent our children. Many of us begin learning about parenting long before our babies are born; we buy books, talk to others and enroll in a variety of parent/child classes. Later, as our children mature, we become their best coaches as well as their loudest cheerleaders.

For that reason, parents will always be a child's first and primary teacher. Parents are most effective because they teach from what they know best—their own experiences personally related to their very favorite pupil. Those few parents who have been formally trained to relate well to children (for example, educators, pediatricians, etc.) have obvious advantages; others who have not been around children until they had them may feel less comfortable relating to them.

Luckily, most parents fall somewhere in between and do a good job of raising their children. The majority of our society is comprised of productive, moral citizens, and most of our children grow up to be law abiding and happy. Obviously, we parents do most things right. However, many of today's parents aspire to be more than just "right"—they strive to be perfect. They rationalize that the more perfectly they parent their children, the more perfect their children will become. Tragically, such pragmatic logic cannot be applied to the business of raising children—it complicates the natural order of family life.

Teaching Children Values for Success

Obviously, children learn a lot by parental example. How parents live and the values they embrace help set the foundation for a child's entire life. It is critical therefore, that parents provide the most positive examples possible for their children to emulate.

Successful children have solid values, understand their purpose and don't compromise on them. Their good values enhance their ability to succeed in and out of school, not distract or misdirect them. Strong appropriate values are so important to a child's success in life that they require not only parent's careful attention, but scutiny. Parents must take the time to examine exactly which values they personally consider most important and demand priority as well as look at which ones should be reconsidered in light of the effect they may have on their child.

Below are two different exercises related to assessing parental values. You may want to do one or both of them to help you better understand how your own values affect your child.

Values Exercise # 1. Rank the values you want most for your child from 1 (most important) to 18 (least important). If possible, both parents should rank the values list separately.

COMMON VALUES

Rank the following values in the order you want your *child* to embrace them:
           1 = most important
           18 = least important

_____ Ambitious (hard-working, aspiring)
_____ Broad minded (open minded)
_____ Capable (competent, effective)
_____ Cheerful (light-hearted, joyful)
_____ Clean (neat, tidy)
_____ Courageous (standing up for your beliefs)
_____ Forgiving (willing to pardon others)
_____ Helpful (working for the welfare of others)
_____ Honest (sincere, truthful)
_____ Imaginative (daring, creative)
_____ Independent (self-reliant, self-sufficient)
_____ Intellectual (intelligent, reflective)
_____ Logical (consistent, rational)
_____ Loving (affectionate, tender)
_____ Obedient (dutiful, respectful)
_____ Polite (courteous, well mannered)
_____ Self-controlled (restrained, self-disciplined)

SOURCE: Sidney Simon, Leland Howe and Howard Kirschenbaum, *Values and Clarification: A Handbook of Political Strategies for Teachers and Students,* Hart, 1972.

Think about what you are doing to demonstrate the importance of each value to your child. How important *should* each value be in your life and in your child's? How important are they presently? After ranking the list, review the values you regard as most important. Are there similarities among the values you live out and those you ranked highest?

Finally, if possible, compare your list with the other parent's list. Do your values correlate or clash? Many parents find the results of this exercise surprising and revealing.

A child's father, for example, may regard intellectualism and ambitiousness as the two most important values on his value scale, while the child's mother may regard politeness and helpfulness as the two most important on hers. To the extent your values significantly differ, who should your child most closely follow?

Children find confusion and conflict over which values to regard as important when they are not demonstrated in meaningful ways. Is the child of the parents in the above example supposed to strive to be hard working or well-mannered, intelligent or helpful?

The value scale can be especially helpful to parents of unsuccessful children because it encourages a closer look at the values and priorities parents most want their children to perceive as important. The scale also can serve to help parents understand how their values and priorities are reflected in their personal life styles.

Values Exercise # 2. Compile a list on paper of personal values (in any order). Parents should make separate lists and then compare them. Discuss how the values between parents are similar as well as different. Reflect on how children might perceive the value messages that each parent conveys.

The primary objective of performing either of the above exercises is to demonstrate that the more specific parents' values are to themselves, the clearer the value messages will be received by their children. Because parents can become so consumed with the demands of daily living, values easily can become confused with wishes and desires. The most effective parents know which values are important and do not compromise on them, resulting in no confusion of them with children.

It is necessary to openly share your thoughts about values as well as consistently demonstrate your good values for your children to model. Realize though that when they grow up your children will exercise the option of either accepting or rejecting all or some of your values. They are, after all, unique individuals and may at maturity have different beliefs and needs for their life.

Learning Attitudes

As the child's first and best teacher, it is parents who stand in the best position to influence children's attitudes about school and learning, positively or negatively. Parental attitudes toward learning and school directly affect the resulting success their children will discover while in school. Parents who have seen positive results from education, for instance, pass their enthusiasm about school and learning onto their children. Conversely, those parents who did not find school pleasant or successful pass their negative or disinterested attitudes to their children.

As a parent, reflect on how your own attitudes toward learning, as with other attitudes, serves to enlighten or prejudice your child because they will affect them lifelong.

Consequently, the resulting attitudes and experiences children have with school affect the feelings they will have about learning (even as adults). They, in turn, will most likely pass their learning attitudes onto the next generation of learners and the cycle will continue, positively or negatively.

Parents who expect their children to do well in school reap the benefits of seeing them try harder and set more challenging goals for themselves. Children's learning successes will not only prove personally rewarding but help lead them to greater self-confidence, curiosity, and an increased faith in taking the risks to learn even more new things.

Teaching Positive Attitudes About Authority and Discipline

Parents hold the major responsibility for teaching their children appropriate attitudes about authority and discipline. These issues cannot be addressed for the first time when a child reaches school age and has difficulty with them—by then it would already be too late to be very meaningful. The child who learns early to respect authority and recognize the positive effects of discipline is a better adjusted student and ultimately a happier person. Students who live by freewheeling, undisciplined standards at home and strict disciplinary and authoritative guidelines at school become confused and anxious. This often leads to angry feelings—and rightfully so.

To avoid such upsets, parents must model sensible standards of discipline and a respect for authority (in all forms) throughout a child's life. Children can be taught such values in a positive and nonpunitive manner so they can ease into school routines with a greater sense of purpose.

Don: It wasn't that Don really caused his teachers and parents any grave problems. Instead, it was the little things that aggravated them, as well as prevented Don from finding school the successful experience it should have been. The middle school years had been bad enough, but now when many of Don's friends were beginning to take on added responsibilities and manage the demands of high school, Don just seemed to be getting worse.

He rarely got up on time, so he was frequently late to

school, and he usually did not complete his homework by the time it was due. Sometimes it wasn't done at all. Other times he coerced his parents into helping him, even though he had the skills to accomplish it independently.

The last straw was when Don was given a second-chance exam in science to help keep him from failing his junior year. It had been a take-home exam and a kind gesture on the part of his concerned teacher. But Don handed it in a day late, as his teacher explained upon answering the door of her house when Don arrived one evening at 10:30 P.M. Don politely apologized for the late exam, as well as for the unexpected late call. He had thought he'd have enough gas in the car to make it, but he ran out on the way to the teacher's house.

His mother was furious when she drove to rescue him from the teacher as well as the stalled car late that night. "I *told* you to finish that test on time, just like I told you to put gas in the car," she exclaimed. Once again he responded by apologizing politely. Don was very sorry about everything—sorry, indeed.

Don may be a "typical teenager" in many respects, but where were the good values of discipline and respect for others Don obviously needed to learn in order to be more successful with home and school? Why had he not learned them earlier in his life?

Appreciating the Uniqueness of Each Child

Every child is born an individual; each shows signs of that uniqueness even before birth. Some children, for instance, are prenatally active; others are very quiet. Some are born large, others small. Each is born with unique traits, just like his or her fingerprints.

Successful parents quickly learn, even with infants, to accept and respect their children as the unique individuals of worth they are. They treat them respectfully, accept both their strengths and inadequacies, and appropriately direct each. Perhaps most importantly, they accept any inadequacies or shortcomings as part of their child's interesting uniqueness.

Expressing Love to Encourage Success

Although parenting can be difficult, demanding and hard on one's patience, it is certainly not without its rewards. Parents have the unique privilege of expressing love to their children in many natural ways that make both parents and children feel well connected and secure. Conversely, where open expressions of love are rare between families, both children and parents feel unloved, thus promoting negative feelings of mistrust and insecurity, especially for young children.

Consider some comments of parents of suicidal children. Many typically wish that they had been more demonstrative in expressing love to their children. Others believe that they did not tell their troubled child of their love and pride often enough or convincingly enough.

Unsuccessful troubled children can easily perceive that their lack of school success influences their parents' love for them. Because unsuccessful children can be extra sensitive and overly serious, they need to know more than ever that they are cared *about*, not just cared *for*. The more parents act in caring ways towards children, especially when they are unsuccessful, the more they learn to care about themselves, and eventually how they succeed in school.

One sure way to show unsuccessful children support is to regularly reach out and touch them. Children of all ages, including teenagers, need lots of loving physical signs—such as hugs, smiles, winks, tickles and kisses by *both* parents.

The relationship between parents and children is such a naturally loving one. Children learn that they are loved, lovable, cared for and capable through strong family ties. Unsuccessful children, unfortunately, do not always have such strong, positive feelings about themselves or their family relationships. So much depends on you.

A WORD TO PARENTS

Vivian Merriman

"I got two A's," the small boy cried.
His voice was filled with glee.
His father very bluntly asked,
"Why didn't you get three?"
"Mom, I've got the dishes done!"
The girl called from the door.
Her mother very calmly said,
"And did you sweep the floor?"
"I've mowed the grass," the tall boy said,
"And put the mower away!"
His father asked him, with a shrug,
"Did you clean off the clay?"
The children in the house next door
Seem happy and content
The same things happened over there,
But this is how it went.
"I got two A's," the small boy cried.
His voice was filled with glee.
His father proudly said, "That's great!
I'm glad you live with me!"
"Mom, I've got the dishes done!"
The girl called from the door.
Her mother smiled and softly said,
"Each day I love you more."
"I've mowed the grass," the tall boy said,
"And put the mower away!"
His father answered him with much joy,

"You've made my happy day!"
Children deserve a little praise
For tasks they're asked to do,
If they're to lead a happy life,
So much depends on you.

How Parental Pushing Affects Children in School

For all its wonderful benefits, parenting is not a job in which one easily finds success. Few parents have any formal training and all parents have their shortcomings.

Many of today's parents are highly educated and successful people who have seen first hand positive results from their own past academic accomplishments and their lives are rich because of their achievements. Unfortunately, some of these same parents secretly regard having children as another great accomplishment and they expect them to be as successful as themselves.

Because they have been successful (or, perhaps, fearing failure), parents have come to expect their children to be either intellectually gifted, physically attractive, extraordinarily athletic—or even have all of these traits! Each achievement the child demonstrates, even as a baby, is viewed as a step toward success, and a successful child is perceived as a "chip off the old successful block."

Sadly, our children have been caught in this crossfire of our success-oriented society. Parenting, therefore, has taken a curious twist from the role of *protecting* children to that of *preparing* them. Today's parents are not just satisfied with guarding and guiding their children as in past generations. Instead, they see their role as preparatory, and the best preparation for success is to provide the children with as many "advantages" as possible. This usually includes overindulgence of material possessions or excessive attention of parent's time.

The results of such "advantages" are that many modern parents (in constantly increasing numbers) indirectly and unconsciously push their children too hard and too fast. Through "loving" attention and interest, children are expected to respond by achieving more and faster. Their diligent efforts are too often motivated by trying to seek the loving approval of their overly involved parents instead of learning for personal intrinsic value.

Teaching About the Rewards of Work

The education of a child is an investment of time, money and immeasurable energy. In part, formal education serves to prepare us for the jobs and careers that await students long after schooling has been completed. Becoming "educated," as with anything, is hard work for some, easy for others. It serves no useful purpose to try to protect children from the hard work that they begin to experience as early as school, but many parents try.

Out of love, most parents try to remove their young child from any stress they can. It is not comfortable watching your child struggle, especially in school, but by having faith in a child's good abilities both parent and child can feel happier and more secure about the total educational process.

Although the "work" of learning in school can be challenging at times, it must be accomplished as much as possible by children themselves. No one can make any child learn. Teachers, parents and peers can provide numerous learning experiences, but in the end it is up to the child to decide what and how to learn. It is must be impressed upon children that it is their choice as well as their responsibility.

Motivating Children

A parent's role in motivating their child in school endeavors should be primarily one of supportive encouragement toward self motivation, not one of provoking added childhood anxiety. Children best learn self-motivation after first having successfully experienced joint cooperation with their parents and other family members.

Motivation is a trait that eventually must grow from within a child. It is the desire to find satisfaction in endeavors by performing well for oneself. Self motivation is critical to school success, but it is not a trait that can be easily taught in the classroom by the teacher.

How does a parent, then, teach an unmotivated child to become self-motivated? Successful parents and teachers use patience and effective communication as their greatest tools. They show respect for the child by avoiding excessive demands or harsh judgments. They guide the child to discover the logical consequences of actions, first at home and then at school.

Controlling or overprotecting children rarely allows them enough opportunities to learn by firsthand experiences the cycle of logical consequences to events—that there is a reaction (or consequence) for every action one makes. When children feel in good control and view their lives as understandable first, then predictable second, they naturally become self-motivated.

Setting Success-Oriented Examples for Children

Children are the greatest imitators. They learn best by the examples set by others around them. There are many people who touch and influence children's lives, but by far the most important are parents.

The appropriate daily examples contributed by parents help shape a child's behavior throughout life. Consider the following questions that convey the ways parents directly affect their child's attitudes and behaviors which influence their success in school.

- Does my child witness me telling the truth even when it is uncomfortable?
- Does my child perceive me as essentially honest in everything I do?
- Does my child see parents who enjoy spending time together rather than in separate activities?
- Does my child see parents in loving relationships who display affection and respect for their partner?
- Does my child observe me giving to others, not only money but also time and concern?
- Does my child see me put less emphasis on material possessions than on people?
- Does my child witness me actively involved in outside interests and hobbies?
- Does my child notice me reading for pleasure when I have free time?
- Does my child observe me working diligently at my job even when I am tired?
- Does my child understand that my love sometimes makes me say "no," which does not mean that I disrespect, reject or do not love him or her?

Children who are successful in the classroom usually have experienced good examples in their home, while unsuccessful children are very often uncertain about which values and examples to follow. Some children may react to such conflict by negating parental values and eventually embracing different ones of their own.

Chris: Chris was a happy guy most of the time. During times of conflict, though, he knew only one way to solve problems. This morning had been one of them.

Timmy had claimed Chris was out at third base while Chris claimed he was safe. Instead of turning to the umpire to state the judgment, Chris immediately threw himself at Timmy and began pounding him on the sidelines. After the fight was broken up by the teacher, Chris was sent inside to the office to quietly await the appropriate disciplinary action.

The principal called Chris into his office, commented on the number of complaints he had heard about Chris's aggressive behavior, and proceeded to suspend him from recess for the remainder of the week. Chris stormed back to class ready to attack Timmy the first chance he got.

Did Chris learn any lesson from this experience? What important values has he learned at home that help him resolve a conflict? If those values don't serve him well when he needs them, how will he feel about those who taught them to him? How will he feel about himself? Right now he is just angry and aggressive.

Parental Beliefs and Academic Achievement

Parental attitudes, expectations and values appear to be closely linked to the causes and effects of children's academic achievement in school. Parents who are well-educated and from academically achieving surroundings appear to have many advantages. Many appear more self-confident and feel more solidly connected to the larger world because of the higher level of understanding they have achieved, mainly through education. But there also appear to be disadvantages. Achievement-oriented individuals also easily get caught up in struggles to find a successful place in this world.

Children, too, learn to mirror the same attitudes of struggling to succeed in a goal-oriented environment. The value of getting good grades at school, for example, too frequently ends up with a child earning solid grades but without much learning. Overemphasizing to a child that good grades implies assurance of a successful job or admittance to an outstanding college can be a false assumption.

Parents who have succeeded themselves know well that it requires hard work to get there and a constant struggle to remain on top. The negative side effects of the long hours, preoccupation and stress that are associated with success are often the high prices people pay for the material rewards and security. Those side effects can affect the whole family in negative ways as well.

Sadly, many of these same "successful" parents push their children to do not only as well as they are capable, but better than they as parents have done, even though they intellectually recognize the flaws of this attitude.

Such seductive values as career goals, lifestyles, drives and desires should be carefully evaluated before pushing them on to children. Career success, after all, does not insure anyone of lifelong happiness; its only guarantee is a different set of demands.

Setting Appropriate Expectations of Children

Unrealistically high parental expectations suggest perfectionism as the standard to children. For children who are trying hard to be successful in school and finding it more difficult each day, such expectations only teach them that they can never expect to achieve them. Children's reactions to such pressure vary from feelings of anger or frustration to various forms of misbehavior at home or school.

In *The Hurried Child*, Dr. David Elkind explains how children can become receptacles of their parents' needs to escape stress themselves and bolster their own self-steem through their precocious son or daughter. We see clear evidence of this fact when we observe the growing number of parents who try to teach their children to read, enroll them in sophisticated classes or music lessons at age three or earlier, or push them into organized sports before they are physically mature enough to handle it. Simply put, there is less emphasis today placed on the value of relaxing, when in reality, because of our fast-paced world, there should be more.

Some children, especially unsuccessful ones, feel that the only way they are truly appreciated by parents and others is to be able to claim some special accomplishment. If they can't, they view themselves as worthless. Parents know that children are separate beings from them and should respect them as such. However, deep inside, an increasing number of parents believe that if their children are less than exceptional as readers, athletes or musicians, it reflects on them personally.

The parent who feels embarrassed or uncomfortable about his child's shortcomings may need to evaluate those personal feelings. Parents whose self-esteem is healthy and strong take pride in their child's *attempts* at any endeavor and do not focus primarily on accomplishments.

Children of high-achieving parents learn by example to expect to be the best. They therefore can sometimes be unrealistic about setting lofty goals and then worry about not being able to achieve them, making many very capable children feel incapable of negotiating such goals successfully. They may have heard numerous times, "You can be anything you want to be—you can be the best!" If the basic expectation is to always be the *best*, how can anyone ever feel hopeful about small, ordinary accomplishments?

Parents who overemphasize the accomplishments of their children also risk giving them false feelings of importance. Most often, such overindulged children do not receive the exclusive attention in a classroom that they have grown used to having at home. This contrast of attention can produce upsetting results because once again the values of the home and school are too diverse. Feeling "entitled" can prevent children from cooperating well in group situations and create great confusion about their real worth, thus resulting in potentially unsuccessful school experiences for unnecessary reasons. Consider Lee's dilemma.

Lee: Lee had been identified "gifted" at the end of third grade. He demonstrated great ability in the area of mathematics and abstract reasoning on the specific "gifted" tests. He also had shown good reading ability and creative thinking. However, throughout the testing situation, Lee also demonstrated how much he hated taking the time to write down those creative thoughts in meaningful ways. Lee, therefore, did not test well on the written part of the "gifted" exam.

His parents learned of the high test scores in math and reasoning during the summer and naturally felt proud. They celebrated the results with Lee and devoted a lot of time to telling him how special he was, especially in the area of math. It wasn't until the fall that they found out that Lee's new placement was in a regular fourth grade class.

The "gifted" committee voted not to invite Lee into the separate gifted class offered at his school, feeling he would not be able to handle the demanding written work.

Lee's parents were devastated when they learned of the decision. Lee felt angry and betrayed. After all, he had been told how special he was all summer long.

So he entered his new fourth grade class in September outfitted with new notebooks and a new stubborn attitude about school— the right ingredients for guaranteeing fourth grade failure.

Parental Attention

Overindulged children honestly believe they are more special than others. This attitude can begin as early as infancy when parents begin to center their attention (almost exclusively) on their baby. Many hope that such attention will be a great advantage later, particularly in school. Some parents eventually grow tired of giving such demanding attention as their children get older, often just when their children need it the most—when they are struggling in school.

When children are showered with over attention, they learn to be self-centered. When they receive too little attention, they feel worthless. Some busy, over-committed parents inwardly feel irresponsible about not being able to give their children the proper balance of quality/quantity time. They vacillate from giving under attention to over attention, very often because of the guilt over their own demanding lives.

Other parents spend exaggerated time and attention on their children secretly hoping that it will help them achieve more outstanding academic performance. When their children don't, such parents become upset, often blaming themselves first. A child's performance in any activity is *not*, as so many parents fear, a reflection of their ability. No child or parent is perfect, and parents should not judge themselves (or feel they are judged) by how well their children perform. In school, a child's performance (especially grades) is only one indication of academic accomplishment at a particular time with a specific skill, and is always changing as new skills are learned.

What children need most to be successful is an appropriate amount of attention geared towards support and understanding—and less in excessive attention and things. Too much or too little attention can be confusing and unfair to a child of any age. Quality and quantity time are equally important to children. However, when parents are not adequately aware of balancing the time and attention they give their children, they end up not giving them enough of either. As a result, both the child *and* parents may feel unsuccessful.

Truly successful individuals live with respect for themselves and others and in synchronicity with the world around them.

Conditional Love Yields Poor Success

The special attention children need they get from many sources. But the attention they find most meaningful is that from family. A job well done becomes a celebration when the positive recognition is from an important family member. It could be attention from a parent, a favorite uncle or a special grandparent. Sometimes, however, that special attention be-comes misconstrued. It is not that the attention is unpositive but instead more conditional, meaning that the demonstra-tions of family praise and love are selectively attached to achievement.

Children from such families learn quickly that the way to be loved and recognized most is to accomplish something special. Children raised with such attitudes learn to believe that their less-than-perfect or less-than-interesting accomplishments (particularly in school) represent almost worthless efforts. When this attitude exists, the joy of learning quickly becomes sublimated by the act of attempting to achieve special recog-nition.

The need to be unusually special puts too much pressure on young students. When children feel their identity is linked more with what they can do than who they are, they can become acutely stressed. Their focus on the fears of failing to be outstanding produces strong negative feelings of self-esteem that can prove devastating for any child, successful or unsuc-cessful.

CHILDREN LIVE WHAT THEY LEARN

If a child lives with criticism,
He learns to condemn.

If a child lives with hostility,
He learns violence.

If a child lives with ridicule,
He learns to be shy.

If a child lives with shame,
He learns to feel guilty.

If a child lives with encouragement,
He learns confidence.

If a child lives with praise,
He learns to appreciate.

If a child lives with fairness,
He learns justice.

If a child lives with security,
He learns faith.

If a child lives with approval,
He learns to like himself.

If a child lives with acceptance and
friendship,
He learns to love the world.

SOURCE: By Dorothy Law Nolte. Taken from Zig Ziglar, *Raising Kids in a Negative World*, Nashville: Thomas Nelson Publishers, 1985, pp. 84-85.

Managing the Gift of Giftedness

The trend toward recognizing the potential "giftedness" in each child not only has received special attention in schools in recent years, but also has raised new issues for educators as well as parents.

The idea of identifying "gifted" children implies that they are very special children—exceptional from other children. Realistically, there are very few people who are truly gifted. For most of us, it is difficult to be gifted in even one area. Nevertheless, many people are "gifted" in some area some of the time, and most people are *very capable* of performing well (although not considered "gifted") in many areas most of the time.

Each individual has the potential for some degree of unique giftedness. Parents should be on the lookout for that uniqueness within their child and turn that potential into talents in natural ways without pressuring them to excel.

Presently, student reaction to the pressures of being identified as "gifted" in school suggests a trend of our children becoming more competitive in an already competitive world. School systems, reacting to increasing pressures from outside the school environment, attempt to acknowledge the special abilities of all children through diagnostic testing and special programs. This pressure, once again, unfortunately, too often reflects more parents' own needs to feel "special"—having special children in special schools than producing better quality education for all children.

Children deserve a respectful attitude from the adults around them about all of their abilities and achievements. They rely on our good judgment to help guide them toward success into adulthood. Is it really fair for so many of us as average achieving adults to expect our children to be so extraordinarily special?

CHAPTER 6

Preparing Your Baby for School

Learning anything new is a process of receiving new information, making sense of it, and then using it in meaningful ways. Learning is an ongoing process that is not limited to merely gaining information or mastering skills; it encourages discovery, stimulates creativity and tickles our imagination, so as to allow us to make better sense of our world. The quest for learning is a basic human trait. We begin learning at birth— with some recent evidence of learning even in the womb— and we are always learning as long as we are living.

A child's first successful learning experiences usually occur in the home. If the home environment is relaxed and loving, as well as stimulating, a child's potential for learning is usually greatly increased. Conversely, if the home environment is disjointed, chaotic or rigid, a child will not feel free enough to learn in such surroundings.

How Children Learn

In school, when teachers recognize that a student is experiencing difficulty in learning, they usually first encourage the

107

distressed student to tap into as many natural resources as possible. All of us have natural resources in the form of our five senses, and we tend to use our strongest senses to enable us to learn in the easiest and most meaningful manner.

Educators refer to the ways children accommodate to different modes of learning as "learning modalities." When teaching, they try to focus on the most effective modalities given the material and children learning it—especially if any children are experiencing difficulty.

Tapping into good natural strengths is fundamental to any successful student. For example, children who rely mostly on their visual sense for information (i.e., they take information into their brains primarily through the use of their eyes), are usually visual learners. For many children (and adults), learning new things visually is the easiest and most lasting way. Learning words by sight, following blackboard work, and completing writing assignments are generally most comfortable for visual learners to manage.

Children who learn best by hearing new information are called auditory learners. There can be about as many children who learn best this way as by the visual approach. Auditory learners usually enjoy such academic challenges as phonics, spelling, oral directions, lectures and films (principally the sound portion).

Of course, in some cases either a visual or an auditory approach works best—depending on the item to be learned—regardless of which is usually their strongest modality. Most often, a combination of visual and auditory modalities are employed by children to help them learn comfortably.

Parents can typically tell which learning modality their child favors by simply observing them in daily activities.

Chase: Chase answers the telephone and remembers the message by simply hearing it. He may need to repeat it to himself several times, out loud or in a mumble, but he seems to be able

108

to hold onto that new information best through his auditory (hearing) channels.

Erika: In contrast to Chase, his older sister Erika hears a telephone message, tries hard to remember it, but then quickly realizes that it is too difficult or frustrating to remember. As a result, she grabs a pencil and tries to write the message down, even if it is just a symbol or a few words. Erika apparently must see the information visually to help herself remember the message best.

The children in both of these examples function well, although differently. Neither way is best or right except that it is best or right for *each* individual.

Still other children need to hear, see and even touch simultaneously in order to learn best. (Recall how babies seem to need to look, feel, touch and taste everything they contact.) These children bring another important modality into focus—the kinesthetic or touching modality. Touching something helps solidify new concepts more thoroughly than just seeing or hearing it. Feeling sandpaper, for example, helps young children better understand the concept of "rough," just as blowing dandelions demonstrates "windy," and stepping in mud certainly explains "squishy" quite well.

Many young children need to be provided with lots of "hands on" or manipulative experiences, for example, in lieu of or in addition to traditional visual or auditory teaching methods. They may need to use as many of their senses as possible to help them understand unfamiliar concepts. This is especially true if the information they are trying to learn is complex.

In time, most children learn well. Nevertheless, at certain times, alternative approaches—such as clipping magazine pictures, watching films or using tangible objects to grasp concepts—may need to be considered to de-emphasize the difficulty of learning something new and instead emphasize the fun of new discoveries.

How do you know when your child is "ready" to learn? Take your cues from your child. Children of all ages act "itchy" and almost bothersome when they are "turned on" to learning something meaningful. They are enthusiastic and insatiably curious about subjects they want to learn.

Bruce: Bruce had not been much of a reader during elementary school. He preferred playing basketball and skateboarding with the boys on his block, but he did okay in school, too. Recently, however, he had developed an interest in sports cars and couldn't seem to get enough information about them.

You could find Bruce curled up in a favorite chair with stacks of magazines, books, brochures, pictures and newspapers all around him. He appeared oblivious to the world and often lost track of time. He was in a world of his own.

His mother just shook her head. "I used to have to nag him to read, now he has to be nagged to do something else. Can anyone understand kids today?" she mumbled, as she vacuumed around both Bruce and his clutter.

Do your children rarely act like Bruce? When it comes to learning, are they quite the opposite instead—acting bored, detached or even resentful toward learning? If so, don't give up, consider instead exploring alternative methods for learning new things.

In school, a variety of methods are employed by teachers to instruct our children. We are indeed fortunate that educators respect the necessity for individualizing our children's instruction. Most frequently, a multisensory approach to learning is encouraged in classrooms, especially with young children. Thus, a variety of options for learning is offered to help our children effectively grasp new information and hold onto it.

Volumes have been written on how to work best with children—how to understand them and how to provide the most enriching educational environment for them. Early successful learning experiences assure children of a solid foundation for later learning. After a string of early successes, which begin in the home, formal learning in the classroom can more easily become meaningful year after year.

Unfortunately, early learning environments that are not enriching for young children frequently do not provide enough opportunities for them to develop curiosity and interest in learning. Both are necessary ingredients, however, for long-lasting school success. Consequently, many stifled students unnecessarily end up unsuccessful in school especially as they grow older.

Project Head Start, the well-known early educational program, was funded by the U.S. Government primarily to provide activities for very young children. The activities were designed (through extensive research) to give young disadvantaged children enriched learning experiences prior to kindergarten so their chances for school success in subsequent years would be greatly increased.

The Mad Rush to Teach Children

Clearly, the more we understand how children grow, the better able we are to help them to learn. In infancy, babies grow rapidly, faster than at any other time in their lives. Therefore, we know that infancy is one of the most important learning times for children. During this period, children begin to develop their basic attitudes about life—including relationships with people and attachments to things.

Early successful experiences help babies make sense of a big world and give them the confidence to want to learn even more new things. However, too many overzealous and overanxious parents attempt to hurry their babies through certain basic childhood-development stages that are pivotal to school success years later.

All stages of childhood growth (physical, mental, emotional and spiritual) are in fact developmental. They are like stair steps: each one must be climbed in order to reach the next and none can be climbed too quickly. In order to find meaning and success at any stair step, a baby must have been comfortable and successful with learning at all previous steps. That is why the learning stages are called developmental.

Sometimes a baby's developmental learning is quite rapid, so rapid that parents may watch their young child make good progress right before their eyes. Other times, developmental learning appears to be rather slow and difficult, thus causing many parents to worry that something is wrong. Erratic growth and learning, however, is very typical with all children, especially when very young. Growth in learning occurs, as with physical growth, sometimes in great spurts, other times in lags.

It is very normal for children to learn some skills quickly while lagging with others. Lagging, or learning at a somewhat slower rate, usually does not imply that children have serious difficulties in learning. It most often means that they need time to progress through a particular stage of learning or with care. It also usually means that they are learning very well. Generally, there is no need for real parental concern.

Many educators believe that the teaching of academic skills should be either delayed until children are older or taught to them at a somewhat slower pace. By following these procedures, children would have the opportunity to learn better because of the additional experiences they would have to draw upon at an older age, or due to the added time devoted to their learning at an earlier age.

Growing up must take its natural course; it cannot be forced or rushed. Rushing children to learn skills has never fostered precociousness, but it can cause havoc inside most children, thus leading to the cycle of anxiety discussed in Chapter 3.

Parents who truly wish to make a significant difference in their children's long-term learning will not push them to learn skills before they are ready, willing and able. Instead, they will encourage them to "flower" in a manner that fosters good feelings of genuine success, not feelings of achievement anxiety. Then they can look forward to succeeding with other endeavors, outside of school and lifelong, banking on the same positive attitude that previously helped them learn so well.

FLOWERING CHILDREN

Children, like flowers, should be free to grow and unfold at their own rate. A classroom of children is like a vase of fresh flowers; they are all different. Some are tall, colorful and strong; others are small, dainty and fragile. Some blossom quickly, others take much longer. Most children, like flowers, resemble the daisies. But some are long-stemmed roses and a select few are even orchids. Nevertheless, they are all beautiful, living organisms, capable of contributing much beauty to our world.

Parents frequently become upset if their children appear to lag with learning specific skills during the first few years of school. They theorize, for example, that children who begin kindergarten as capable readers not only have a head start in formal learning, but also will continue to progress at the same rapid rate throughout their school career. Curiously, just the opposite is more often true. Most kindergartners who enter school reading "above grade level" tend to level off at some point. They slow down and settle into a learning pace that is not only comfortable but stimulating.

A "rushed" child becomes an anxious child, and eventually grows uncomfortable and weary of such a frantic learning pace. Many children cease trying to maintain the pace and give up, often when learning should be the most fun.

Parents who do not allow their children to find a pace at which they can comfortably succeed in school, place too much pressure on them. Stressed children have seen the highs and lows of school success—and the price of it. They have concluded that learning is neither very much fun nor worth the effort. These children can simply "burn out"—some as early as third grade. How perceptive a child can be. And what a quick learner!

In contrast, most unpressured children who enter kindergarten or first grade as non-readers learn skills in a more natural, progressive way. They delight and find great satisfaction in learning something for the very first time. Thus, they become discoverers. They see skills unfold naturally in the exciting place they know as school. These happy and relaxed children progress at a steady rate. They find success with their learning and look forward to new challenges and grades in school.

Ironically, by grade three—typically a good grade to evaluate educational ability and progress—most parents cannot tell which children began kindergarten reading "above grade level" and which had not learned about reading at all. Interestingly, however, it is almost always apparent which children were pushed into early learning experiences before they were ready. They are usually the students who have become victims of the early pressures and have given up on learning.

Parents and Children Learning Together—Successfully

The unique relationship between parents and children is a delicate one. Parents and children learn about each other as they both grow and mature. Parents who are in close touch with their child when they are young are usually well aware of how and when their learning needs change as they grow older. Caring parents demonstrate love for their children through respect for their individuality, recognition of their needs and encouragement of their efforts. They support them best by guiding them through new experiences. They foster independence by encouraging them to make their own choices along the way. They allow their children the freedom to make mistakes without the fear of retribution.

The most successful parents also have plenty of confidence in their own parenting abilities. A by-product of that confidence is their ability to relax and *enjoy* watching their children grow and learn about their new world. Parents' confidence greatly influences their children's own confident attitudes in school because children are such natural imitators of parents.

Parents who read regularly for pleasure in front of their children, for example, give them the subtle message that reading is an enjoyable and worthwhile activity. Also, they project the attitude that learning is an ongoing activity, even for adults. Such good values about reading (and learning) are essential to school success.

Babies Learning Language

All babies are born with the potential for learning good language skills. One of the best ways they first learn language is by listening to others. Good language skills do not easily take shape without good listening skills. Because babies need to hear and relate to language as early as possible, parents should begin talking to them as soon as they are born. Just because babies can't talk yet does not mean they are unable to process what you're saying. Fine language skills are rated among the most important for guaranteeing school success because without good language skills, good reading cannot easily take shape.

Listening can be encouraged by helping baby become aware of such ordinary sounds as the everyday sounds around your house. Young babies, for instance, can be particularly sensitive to environmental sounds, and from them they learn to begin to make sense of the world around them. To help babies learn about listening, there also are numerous high-quality listening toys available, which provide opportunities for babies to sharpen their listening awareness.

As they grow and mature, babies learn to extend their language beyond positive listening to develop their own voice through babbling. Babbling should be encouraged because it is baby's first way of verbally expressing language.

Since babies are generally incapable of responding to language in recognizable ways, many parents relate to babies as though they are unable to respond at all. This assumption is definitely wrong. Babies need lots of opportunities to interact with language in various intimate ways. The time parents devote to helping babies relate to the world through language (including listening and communicating) will pay off in both short- and long-term rewards.

In conclusion, good language and listening skills are essential for school where they will be used repeatedly in classroom situations at all grade levels. Babies who learn early to regard language and listening as important continue to transfer that same positive attitude to the classroom even many years later.

Guaranteeing Babies a Successful Start

Children learn most rapidly when they are very young. Babies learn more in the first two years than they do in any other period of their lives. Watch babies—most are very willing to try to learn anything. They bring curious minds to any new learning situation. Channeling that positive learning attitude is essential to later success.

Babies learn the entire time they are awake. They are born with an insatiable desire to explore and learn and they use all five of their senses to do it. That is why they stare, listen, touch, taste and smell everything. Parents, as baby's best teacher, can direct this learning obsession in ways that will aid them in school much later.

Babies require a lot of time and space to explore their new world. Babies who are contained in playpens, harnesses, etc., are physically limited in the ways they are able to explore. Of course, at times it is necessary for parents to confine baby for safety reasons or quiet time. But such constraints, when over-used, limit a baby's learning experiences. Remember, all later school learning will be conditional on baby's early learning experiences—free or confined.

Aside from providing positive learning experiences to enhance a baby's school situation later, spending lots of loving, happy and relaxed time with them enhances their learning potential as well. And happy babies become happy students.

Teaching Babies Skills for Success

Most parents like to teach their babies. They enjoy the responsibility of being their baby's first teacher as well as showing baby the things that they as parents find meaningful. Unfortunately, few parents have the advantage of formal training in how to teach baby best.

To get the most from any instructional time you spend with your baby, begin by observing what he or she appears to enjoy doing most during relaxing times; what is stimulating or attractive to them? What activities do they do with ease, and which do they find difficult or frustrating? Use this information to make all "teaching time" worthwhile. But be aware, for instance, that providing a baby with too many toys or distractions can confuse, overstimulate and eventually frustrate them.

Instead of many toys, it is usually best to offer only one stimulation (toy) at a time. As you work with them, use language to expand the interaction with the toy or activity instead of moving on to a new one, and remember that babies need to have things repeated in order to understand and master the skill being learned.

117

Second, think in terms of what your baby's learning needs are when teaching them, not what your desires are for them. And never try, of course, to teach a baby who is tired, sick or hungry. Appropriate teaching time (only for five minutes or so at first) enables a baby to increase interest in learning and feel well connected to the family (i.e., knowing that there are loving, supportive people around them).

Interestingly, by age four, children's IQ (intelligence quotient) becomes rather well established and fairly accurately predicts what it will be even at the age of 17. One can see, therefore, how the ways parents interact with children in the first few years directly influences their future school success. (See bibliography for suggested books on teaching babies.)

How Good Nutrition, Behavior and Learning Interrelate

Most parents understand the importance of good nutrition for their children—how it can affect not only their good health, moods and attitudes, but also their developmental growth. Thus, poor nutrition can cause not only illness but slower learning as well.

The more lags children experience in their early learning (for whatever cause), the more they will be at risk later when they attend school. Adequate developmental learning requires proper physical growth as well as adequate intellectual and emotional growth—all necessary components for school success.

Over the past few years, research has shown how certain foods (or parts of) can cause negative effects on some children's delicate balance of health, moods and overall behavior. The studies also have helped to make parents and teachers alike better aware of how some additives, preservatives, pesticides, artificial colorings and flavorings can affect children's ability to remain focused even in academic settings. When the questionable foods were reviewed and removed from certain

118

children's diets, researchers found that some were better able to concentrate on a task, thus eliminating this hindrance to their good ability to learn.

There are, of course, differing opinions about theories of nutrition and its affects on behavior and learning (hyperactivity and attention deficit disorder, for example). There are many good sources for parents to turn to regarding the relationship between nutrition, behavior and learning. Your doctor or a school nurse can recommend some appropriate materials to read if the subject is of further interest.

Because of the interest in improving children's health and behavior in any possible way, most baby food companies have minimized or eliminated starches, colorings, sugars and salts in their packagings. Parents too, seem to be relying more on fresh foods and more nutritional information to guide them. These positive steps toward awareness of children's nutrition can only help their behavior and success in school.

As an exercise, consider reading the following checklist to further understand the link between good behavior and good learning.

Could My Child Be Hyperactive?

Read the following general characteristics of childhood hyperactivity and check those that apply to your child. Keep in mind that this list is very general and not all inclusive of hyperactive behaviors.

_____ Attends to everything—unable to ignore stimuli
_____ Is continuously in motion, fidgety, unable to sit still
_____ Touches seemingly everything
_____ Has short attention span, moves quickly from one activity to another, leaves projects incomplete
_____ Is easily distractible
_____ Tends to be forgetful

_____ Is aggressive, hostile, irritable or emotional
_____ Dismantles or destroys toys
_____ Has a low threshold for pain, temperature, or tickling—readily laughs or cries
_____ Is overly demanding, insists on things "my way"
_____ Disrupts class, talks during class, or teases other children
_____ Is clumsy
_____ Is impatient
_____ Loses things often
_____ Has nervous habits—such as sucking on blanket or clothes, biting or picking fingernails, or twirling hair
_____ Is accident-prone
_____ Attempts reckless stunts
_____ Interrupts
_____ Talks loudly, excessively, or rapidly
_____ Panics
_____ As a baby, appeared to have colic
_____ As a baby, sucked thumb or pacifier
_____ As a baby, rocked crib
_____ As a baby, banged head when angry.

SOURCE: Barbara Kuczen, *Childhood Stress* (Delacorte Press, 1982), pp. 184-5.

CHAPTER 7

Encouraging Your Unique Young Learner

Why do some young bright children blossom at school while others, who have the same experiences, develop negative attitudes about learning, school and even themselves?

Burton L. White, Project Director at Harvard's Preschool, says in his book *The First Three Years of Life*, "It is during the baby's second year that the behavior of parents begins to differ widely from one family to another. Some encourage baby's curiosity and zest for learning language, while some others speak to their babies more. Other mothers see growth as an expanding danger around the child and, therefore, unfortunately, overprotect the child."

Ideally, most babies begin life with a warm, loving relationship with their mother, then they expand those good feelings to include others around them. They learn to trust—family first, acquaintances next, and eventually strangers and new experiences. Without that solid sense of trust, children can grow up too restricted and inhibited to be able to enjoy new challenges and achieve their personal potential.

As newborns mature to infants and then young children,

they become more and more aware of their growing environment. Through increased awareness they learn to deal with their world in more active, rather than passive, ways. Then through a variety of good experiences, young children begin to learn that the world is a safe and exciting place in which to live.

Learning in Natural Ways

Often, it is during the special times between parent and child that the very best learning occurs—in the most natural ways. Learning can occur through a variety of experiences at work or play, by the child alone or with others, like Robby below.

Robby: Robby, age 5, learned the game well and usually won. His mom called it Grocery Tag and he loved it. The objective of the game was to get exactly what his mother requested in each aisle of the grocery store before she went to the next aisle. "Three yellow apples," she'd say as she checked out the lettuce and rolled on to the other produce.

Robby retrieved the goods in lightning speed and put a point by his name on a piece of paper after she assured him of getting the correct item. As they moved through the store, she increased the level of difficulty of the demands. "Two medium-sized cans of peas with the silver label," she'd challenge. Robby searched through the canned vegetables and came running with two large cans with a white label, so mom got a point that time. Robby's mother not only kept his interest during the family shopping trip, but helped him learn colors, sizes, comparisons and, most importantly, good listening skills—all skills that would serve him well later in school.

Robby "won" that day, so on the way out of the store, he got to choose a prize. He chose a pack of his favorite gum. Lucky boy—in more ways than one.

122

Learning Through Experience

By far the most natural way to expand children's learning is to provide them with as many rich experiences as possible. I began reading to my own child as a baby, as soon as she was able to stay awake long enough to look at a few pictures in a book. She learned firsthand the importance of books, as well as recognizing, through visual stimulation, a connection between objects in a book and objects in her own new world.

Children understand little about the world until they are made more aware of its inner-workings. Therefore, any experiences parents can provide their young children, like Joey below, are not only exciting and new but also beneficial to all future learning.

Joey: Joey's mother listened carefully as the teacher explained the first grade curriculum during the fall parent/teacher conference. The teacher pointed out that Joey did not seem to know many of the basic concepts that most children learn prior to attending school. He acted hopelessly confused over colors, for example, and was even bewildered about the color of the sky. He *must* be comfortable with such basic concepts before being expected to find any relevance to higher-level skills such as reading, she explained.

The teacher suggested ways Joey's mom might help reinforce simple concepts like colors with Joey at home: cutting out all the blue clothes in a magazine, looking for all the blue cars when riding in the car, or even just noticing the blue sky on clear days. Anything that would help make the color blue relevant to Joey would help him get ready to learn to read.

Joey's mother listened carefully to all the suggestions. She thanked the teacher for her time and as she left, she turned back to the teacher and said, "I had no idea Joey didn't know his colors. You know, if Joey had only asked me, I would have told him what color the sky was."

Providing Opportunities for Active Thinking

We recognize that most young children are bright and successful in school. Many are extraordinarily creative, too. Some of our children, however, do not appear to be intellectually challenged enough to develop adequate mental or thinking skills in school. In other words, these children just don't have to think much to get by.

All children, successful or not, need to have their analytical and creative abilities nurtured as early in life as possible. Common diversions such as television or videos generally do not encourage active thinking. Instead, they demand little "involved" thinking while providing strong gratification. With such distractions tempting children, it is once again up to parents to monitor the time spent on them.

In other words, parents who wish to boost their child's thinking more creatively at home should themselves be alert to using more open-ended questions when interacting with their child. For example, Questioning Method A (below), although not bad, does not encourage the depth of thinking required of Questioning Method B.

QUESTIONING METHOD A

Dad: "What color was the polar bear in the story I just read to you, Jan?"

Jan: "White."

QUESTIONING METHOD B

Dad: "Jan, why do you think the polar bear in the story I just read to you is the color he is?"

Jan: "He's white so that he'll blend into the snow."

124

or

"He's white so he'll be like everything else where he lives."

or

"Gee, I never thought about that. I guess I don't know, Dad. Why?"

By using Questioning Method B, diverse levels of thinking are stimulated, more than with Questioning Method A, which tends to limit or even discourage active thinking. Method B can be expanded with children based on their level of ability and understanding. Interestingly, this is another example of how so much of a parent's influence on their child's learning has little to do with their direct involvement with the academic subjects of the classroom. This type of involvement can make positive, powerful differences in school performance, however, as evidenced by the simple questioning examples above.

Encouraging Imagination in Your Child

Using one's imagination should be encouraged with children of all ages. Imaginative tasks spark creativity and encourage inventive thinking. Reflect for a moment on our world without the imagination of Walt Disney, Dr. Seuss or Steven Spielberg, for instance. It would create a tremendous void because of the way they delight and stimulate us all.

Unfortunately, there is not enough time in most formal classroom situations for much pretending and imagining. There are curriculum objectives to meet and other demands on classroom time. Parents must therefore help encourage imaginative thinking. Specific activities, books and toys that are brain teasers or without well-defined solutions, for instance, serve to stimulate a child's imagination.

Unsuccessful children, in particular, need plenty of opportunity for encouraging imaginative thinking. When their mind is preoccupied with worry about schoolwork or themselves, they may feel stifled in their ability to imagine and create.

Learning Through Toys

Traditionally, toys have been an area of great interest as well as considerable conflict for parents. Too frequently, they don't know which toys provide the best learning challenges for their children and which are just a waste of money from a learning viewpoint.

Toys should serve useful purposes and meet specific needs for children, but at the same time still be F-U-N. Toys do not need to be overly expensive or sophisticated. (Young children, for instance, generally can find contentment in simple, everyday objects from the kitchen drawer or closet, etc.) Providing children too many toys can overstimulate them to the point that they are unable to gain meaning from any of them. Children play best with a toy that allows them to interact with it in their world as they understand it.

The most "valuable" toy enables both the toy and the world to take on more meaning for the child.

Young children (ages 3-6) who play with a variety of buttons or colored spools of thread, for instance, learn in a natural way to classify, compare and sort things into logical groups. Young children also are capable of comparing license plates on cars, faces in magazines or sizes of cookies, for example. Similarly, they can discover relationships between the numbers on clocks and those on gasoline pumps, houses, etc. All of these "games" help children learn to be aware as well as skillful, thus they begin to relate to the larger world by making sense out of how things interrelate. (Note that none of the above examples requires expensive, fabricated toys.)

If buying the "right" toy is a puzzle for you—as it is for most parents—try to think of how the toy you are considering will serve a given purpose. What is its "staying power" for your child? How long will he or she find it attractive? One minute? One day? One year? Meaningful relationships between children and their toys help them later with school challenges, primarily because toys help teach children that learning is fun.

Nursery School—A Necessity or a Nemesis?

For many parents, selecting an appropriate nursery school is as complex and stress-provoking as trying to select an appropriate college for a high school student. What really motivates us to such dedication? Why do we seem so compulsive about sending our children to nursery school, and perhaps more importantly, why so soon? Is it really necessary? What will our children learn of value in nursery school? Will it help make them more successful in school later?

In an effective nursery school situation, children learn some basic skills—often through their first group social interactions—while simultaneously learning some independence from parents and the home. This sometimes is not always easy for young children.

Skills that are taught in nursery school are usually thought out carefully and based on solid research in childhood development. The skills taught are matched to children's physical and developmental ages and are among those that will help promote success later in elementary school and in all future developmental stages.

But what about children who appear not to be ready for the complexities of nursery school? What will happen if they go too late? What is the risk if they go too soon when they are not really old enough to have a positive experience?

The result of *any* unsuccessful school experience (at any age) may be that the complex world children enter only can serve to complicate their life instead of adding order to it. Parents need to understand the seriousness of this issue and accept that if a young child is not making sense of any formal school experience, they should immediately consider other alternatives.

Good nursery schools provide experiences that offer excellent teaching models for children. Their activities and methods are thought out with great care, because children learn by imitating and modeling themselves after those around them, including teachers and other's reactions to experiences.

Most nursery schools emphasize immersing young children into extensive language experiences. Educators agree that good language is *the* "prereading" skill to be developed for reading to be successful later. The broader the language base a child has to draw from, the more they are able to learn from and relate to each new experience.

Nursery schools also provide a variety of creative "hands on" experiences because they allow children to discover at their own rate using a multisensory approach. Children are encouraged to "manipulate" or "feel" each new experience, as well as talk about it.

When Is It Best for Children to Learn?

Good teachers don't force children to do what they are unable to accomplish easily; instead they gently encourage them to discover more through each small success. If teachers or parents force children of any age to learn before they are ready, the children will soon look upon all learning as frustrating (even at a very young age) and give up. It is truly sad to watch a curious young child not risk learning something new for fear it is too difficult.

When parents attempt to teach their young child before he

or she is ready, for example, they often encounter strange results. Most children try very hard to learn new skills. They tend to enjoy learning anything new and will even take on added frustration just to please parents. However, with repeated failure, this normally positive learning attitude can soon change. They may act out their learning frustrations in a variety of ways, such as overt misbehavior and withdrawal—at school or at home.

In Project Head Start, the federally-funded nursery school program, the original objective was to provide stimulating preschool experiences for disadvantaged young children, with the hopes that they would be guaranteed better chances for school success later. The theory specifically contrasted with that of waiting until problems occurred to help children when they showed signs of school difficulty. The program continues to have merit today, particularly in its philosophy.

Curiously, experts blame much of the lack of school success of disadvantaged students on their suffering from too few stimuli and experiences in their young lives. In contrast, they fault the lack of school success of advantaged students on too many possessions and not enough direct attention from the important people around them. Both types of children may be labeled as unsuccessful in school, but each may fail for opposite reasons.

In addition, there are other young but unsuccessful school children who have had rich advantages in and out of school. They have had caring parents and teachers who have done many things to help insure their success at school. Unfortunately, because of such loving attention, many of these children may not have learned to act and think independently enough. As a result, when independent expectations are placed on them in formal school settings, they may not succeed with the demands.

Parents (and teachers) should generally not do for children what they are capable of doing themselves. Children must learn independence early in life and experience confidence with their unique abilities, especially those skills vital to school success.

How do you know when your child is "ready" to learn? Take your cues from your child. Eager learners of all ages act "itchy" and almost bothersome when they are "turned on" to learning something meaningful. They are enthusiastic and insatiably curious about subjects they want to learn.

Understanding the Relevance of Reading

Reading is one of those skills "vital" to school success. Therefore, reading with your child is more than important; it is a necessity because it satisfies so many of the needs of children. With young children, reading serves as a special time for learning, listening, relaxing and sharing cherished moments between the child and parent.

Annie: Annie's mother had always read to her for as long as she could remember. Annie recalls it as one of her favorite family times. Sometimes Mom read poems or fairy tales, other times just good old stories.

Now Annie's parents had separated and many of the pleasant family traditions had ceased. It was a sad time for Annie; the world often looked pretty frightening and unpredictable to her, especially at bedtime. It was certainly reassuring when her mom sat down next to her on her bed and opened a book at bedtime.

Annie snuggled down under the blankets as she had always done and let all the "worry thoughts" float away as she took refuge in the world between the pages of the story book. She asked, "Mom, I love bedtime when you read me a story. Will you promise to still read to me when I'm all grown up?"

Precocious Early Readers: A Warning!

Most parents today feel a stronger responsibility to teach their children to read at least a little by a preschool age. Most begin by teaching them to read aloud. They believe that if their child can show evidence of being a fluent reader before kindergarten, that he or she will be at the very least "advantaged," and possibly even "gifted." It then follows that these same parents may expect their child to be considered for accelerated classes, gifted and talented labels, lifelong success and happiness ever after! Experienced teachers know otherwise.

Learning to read is not a simple skill to master or teach. Reading is primarily a thinking process and, like other important milestones, children do not learn to read successfully until they are ready to do so developmentally. This requires physical, emotional and mental growth as well as social maturity. Children learn to read when they are ready, just as they learn to walk and talk when they are ready.

Most parents, no matter how well intended, are not qualified to teach their children how to read *well* for many reasons. They tend, for instance, to grossly underestimate the amount of time, work and psychology that is involved in *successfully* teaching the entire reading process.

Most young children can learn to read some words well enough to appear capable in front of parents or other important people in their lives. As an added bonus, they typically gain plenty of individual attention and are made to feel quite special for their "performances." However, very few young children enter school having any real idea of *what* they are reading. Their understanding of what they read (comprehension) is usually worlds apart from their ability to identify individual words. Primarily, this is because of their young age and lack of extensive experiences, not because of lack of ability. Professionally speaking, early forced rote reading offers neither guarantees of success nor later advantages for any child.

Paul: The Thomases had two young children, Paul and Rachel. Paul was the only child for the first 2½ years of his life. His mother, enthusiastic about the challenge of being the perfect mom, spent a lot of her free time teaching Paul everything she could, especially before Rachel was born.

Now that Paul was 3 years old, Mrs. Thomas sat with her coffee and morning newspaper, seriously considering enrolling Paul in the class that advertised "guaranteeing" to teach young children to read. She was quite amazed at Paul's bright and curious nature, and felt certain he was an unusually precocious child.

One day soon after, Mrs. Thomas approached a teacher friend about her thoughts of the "guaranteed to read" class for young learners like Paul.

The teacher listened quietly. "Tell me more about Paul. What types of things does he like to do?" she asked. "What would he like to read?" the teacher friend asked.

Mrs. Thomas looked shocked. "He doesn't know," she replied, "he's only three."

"You're right," said the teacher. "I feel the same way about someone teaching him to read!"

Many children who learn to read at unusually young ages before kindergarten, enter school with distorted views of themselves or their identities. They see themselves as exceptional, primarily because they have been told so repeatedly by the many trusted people in their world. They frequently act bored or frustrated in a school setting when learning is less than "entertaining" or if they are not treated as "special." As a result, many either lose their motivation for learning or simply "burn out" in higher grades.

132

Also, parents of unsuccessful older students for instance, can frequently act disbelieving if they learn that their "precocious young reader" is no longer succeeding in school. In the higher grades, you'll recall, the workload often becomes more difficult and expanded, and teachers expect more than just simple word identification skills to demonstrate good reading ability.

In addition, early readers do not always learn the reading process *well*; more often, they can perform rote word reading almost perfectly. Thus, when reading tasks become more challenging and demanding of intellectual involvement as the grades progress, many early readers become frustrated and give up. They often feel betrayed by those trusted people who were always telling them how very special they were because of how well they read.

Instead of *teaching* their children to read prior to entering school, what can parents do most to help? The answer is *read, read, read* to your child—every day, and from a variety of materials, including books, magazines, and even the daily mail. In addition, point out road signs, bumper stickers, and even the writing on tee shirts. Make certain, too, that your children have many opportunities to observe *you* reading frequently. Finally, provide even a very young child many opportunities and uninterrupted time each day to explore books and pictures.

Lauren: I never taught my own daughter, Lauren, to read at an unusually young age. As a reading specialist, I was certainly qualified to teach her to read when she was very young, but I made the conscious decision not to. Instead, I used the time that I would have spent in drilling her on words and reading skills exposing her to books and rich literary experiences.

Through books, she learned of the world around her, of exotic animals and far away places. She learned about people's emotions and how to solve problems. She learned to appreciate art, poetry, riddles and humor, as well as enjoy mystery, fairy tales and fantasy. She even slept with her books instead of her toys. They were often her best friends. The greatest lesson she learned, however, was that reading is fun and that the world through books is always exciting and never disappointing.

When she entered first grade as a non-reader, after spending some time in nursery school, she was very eager to learn to read. She was curious and excited. She viewed reading as a way to learn more.

Today, she is considerably ahead of her grade level in reading. She still stumbles over words, but her comprehension is exceptional because her interest in reading remains high, even now. Recently, she has begun to expand her solid reading skills into a more advanced skill—creative writing.

By my teaching her to sit quietly, listen carefully, and verbally react to what was between the pages of books, she saw the process of reading come together in a natural, meaningful way.

I have never regretted not teaching her to read earlier. Instead, I am most proud of the legacy she has been given—an appreciation for reading that will enhance her life forever.

On Entering Elementary School

How do parents promote successful beginnings for their young school child? Their own attitudes about school will be most influential. If parents believe that school is exciting and important, they will pass those positive feelings on to their child.

Entering school is a quantum leap in any child's life. Ask any mother how she felt the day her child began first grade. The expectations and demands of school can be high—children are expected to remain seated for long periods of time, listen attentively and perform sophisticated written tasks. They must also organize an important part of their life independently, usually for the first time for most children.

Some very capable students, especially younger ones, may not be ready at the tender age of six for the mature school experiences expected of them. If they're not ready, it *may* be better to allow them to repeat kindergarten or have a different educational experience. The sad alternative of forcing a child to experience school before he or she is ready may be an educational situation that promises failure as the very first formal school experience.

Tragically, premature education can damage children by permanently altering their "learning attitude." Many learn to believe that they are not smart enough because of failing to succeed so early. It is heartbreaking to watch a bright child become emotionally affected in a negative way by premature education and early pressure to succeed. Their good energy becomes wasted on trying to cope, rather than on trying to learn.

Many educators believe we should delay more basic learning until the end of elementary school when children have more maturity and experiences to draw upon, instead of escalating it in the early years as so many parents seem to prefer.

In the past, holding children back in a grade always implied failure. But today, curiously, there are a growing number of parents who, without basis, *choose* to hold their child back in early grades such as kindergarten or first grade. Their child may or may not have experienced success in school. But if parents fear future failure, they may rationalize that if they give their child more time to mature in kindergarten or another grade, they will be guaranteed more success, both in that and subsequent grades. Such a reckless thinking about school placement could be called "reverse pushing" or "slingshotting."

Parents who push children to perform skills too soon or hold them back to push them later put children, family and even themselves at risk. They should seriously examine their personal value system to determine why their child's early school success is so very important to require such drastic action. (See Chapter 5.)

There is no logic in holding children back with hopes that if given extra time they will be "extra ready." While there sometimes are specific, appropriate reasons for a child's lack of success, in most cases children who are held back a grade do not perform much differently than they would if they had not been held back. This issue of grade retention is discussed at length in Chapter 9.

CHAPTER 8

School—The Child's Workplace

School is the place of work for children. It is where they have their desk, supplies and specific responsibilities. It is, therefore, their "workplace."

Children go to "work" to challenge ideas, solve problems, work cooperatively and discover the internal rewards of learning. As with any job, school can be fun and hard work at the same time. Children (the "workers") frequently are expected to succeed with many unfamiliar concepts. Pressure is often put on them to perform tirelessly at high levels of understanding. For some children, the pressures and frustrations become too great and lead to disinterest in school or even "burnout." (See Chapter 10 on childhood stress and anxiety.)

The Pressure Cooker Classroom

To understand how children feel about their work at school and learning requires understanding what today's classrooms are like. On the one hand, schools are happy, energetic places that encourage learning with intriguing materials and equipment plus competent professionals to direct them. On the other hand, however, they can be demanding environments for both students and teachers.

Today, most teachers are under extraordinary pressure to teach students more, at higher levels and faster rates, while simultaneously showing extra concern for them individually. Teachers are also held accountable for filling out multiple forms for students' attendance, test scores, grades, health and behavior.

Teaching has become such a demanding job with so few rewards that too few of us are now interested in pursuing it as a lifelong career. These negative attitudes directly affect the quality of our children's education.

There can be little time to teach our children skills like functional thinking or organizational methods that will assist them lifelong. The many good teachers who regard these critical skills as important experiences for children can no longer fit the teaching of them into the regular school day. Some complain that they don't even have time to read young children a story or engage in open-ended discussions about current events, much less address simple principles of philosophy and logic. Instead, many teachers surrender to the pressure to cover elaborate curriculum in short time frames in order to increase test scores and keep the school community happy.

The Influence of the Classroom Teacher

Children come into contact with a variety of adults who work directly and indirectly with them during the regular school day. Their main adult model is, of course, their individual teacher(s).

Recognize that, in general, each teacher represents a one-year contribution to your child's life. Outstanding teachers can shape a child's learning to such a degree that they create a

138

lifelong influence on the child. We all remember that handful of teachers who had a great influence on us.

By the nature of the job, a teacher's attention must be divided between numerous students and responsibilities during any school day. There are few occasions when teachers are able to give more than a few minutes of individual attention to any one student. With today's complex educational system, it is unrealistic to expect more. This is why most teachers prefer to teach in small groups.

In any class, teachers also face a variety of individual student challenges that include giftedness, learning disabilities, physical, emotional and cultural differences, as well as a wide variety of learning styles and maturation levels. It is the teacher's goal to extract the best peformance relative to the potential of each child in that classroom. This is a primary challenge driving good teachers to teach, in spite of adverse circumstances.

Being Attentive to Attendance

Children can only be assured of being successful in school when they are attending school regularly. They cannot learn if they are not where the lessons are being taught. Encouraging good attendance costs little time-wise and yields great results.

Far too often, students miss learning important lessons in school to comfort minor pains, sleep in, extend vacations and keep appointments. Although these activities may be necessary, it is the parents' responsibility to make sure that such activities are avoided or minimized during school time. Attendance will only be important to children if first it is important to parents.

Help your child get the necessary rest and nutrition needed so that tiredness and illnesses are minimized. Be respectful of your child's school schedule when making non-emergency medical appointments, and weigh the value of extending a vacation against the new instruction your child will miss while somewhere else.

Managing Time Wisely

The subject of time, including how it serves and constrains us, can become easily misunderstood by an unsuccessful child. Managing time in a wise manner can help make the successful difference for any child who is struggling to balance his or her school responsibilities.

Adults seem to take the concept of time for granted. Children, however, don't. Many seem to lack a general sense of time and need help learning how to tell time before they can be expected to *use* their time wisely, especially in school.

Parents can help most by teaching children to focus on the amount of time everyday activities require by simply stating the concepts verbally to them. For example, "It only takes ten minutes to walk the dog; then you'll still have 30 minutes to shower before your favorite TV show comes on." These verbal "helpers" aid all children, successful and unsuccessful, in making better sense of their world.

Eventually, all children learn to regard time as important, but not necessarily early enough. It sometimes takes awhile, and is another skill they need to begin to learn at home first. Daily routines and schedules for eating, working, playing and sleeping help children learn the sequence of time and ease them naturally into thinking about the relationship time has to their lives. Later they will be better able to transfer that relationship to help them manage their time wisely in school.

Fostering Good Listening Skills

The most common complaint of teachers is that too few children know how to listen well. Children also must develop good listening habits prior to attending school because listening ranks as one of *the* most important skills a child needs to guarantee success in school. Too often, children like Wendy (below) listen selectively, tuning in or out at their discretion and, of course, to their detriment at home and at school.

Wendy: "Wendy, would you run upstairs, find my purse and get a dollar out of my wallet for your little brother to take to school for lunch? The school bus will be here any second now. Please hurry," Mrs. Bond said quickly as she helped little Billy with his raincoat.

Wendy ran upstairs and into her mother's bedroom. She scanned the room for what she needed. Without much thought, Wendy grabbed her mother's car keys and ran downstairs again.

"Here, Mom," said Wendy.

"This isn't what I asked for, Wendy. Didn't you listen? Can't you hear?" Mom shouted as she ran up the stairs herself, hearing the school bus coming up the block.

Many unsuccessful children are unusually poor listeners for a variety of reasons: they may be preoccupied about something, disinterested in a specific subject, hungry, tired, overwhelmed with worry, or just undisciplined. Therefore, any effort parents make at home to encourage sharper listening skills at school will serve to benefit an unsuccessful child. Ask any teacher.

A practical way to begin encouraging sharp listening skills is for parents themselves to be attentive listeners to the child. When a child has something to say, be respectful and look and listen to them in an active way. It usually takes only a small amount of time and patience to reap large benefits. Children will naturally learn by such good examples that listening is valuable both socially and academically.

Secondly, parents, on a consistent basis, should give their child (of any age) simple directions and then expect that they be carried out properly. This approach forces a child to focus on listening for a useful purpose. Like Wendy's mother, many parents who do not get instant results from their efforts give up and complete the tasks themselves. As a result of not following through, they are not demanding good listening skills, and their child stands a chance of never learning to be a good listener.

Assuming that listening to simple directions is mastered effectively, parents should then increase the level of complexity of directions to include multi-step ones (more than two steps). Intricate directions encourage children to listen even more closely in order to follow through more successfully with what they have heard. Their success with these exercises, of course, should be properly praised and not be taken for granted. These more involved types of listening skills are similar to those necessary as a child advances through subsequent grades.

In conclusion, when teachers talk they expect children to listen, remember what they have said, and follow through. There is no room for compromise with listening skills when a teacher is teaching many students. Successful adults often credit their listening ability as being instrumental to their own success and a skill they value in others. Indeed, it must be true, for we all appreciate a person who truly is a good listener.

Reading to Learn

For older students reading can have different demands than for younger children. After elementary school, little classroom instruction time is spent on the mechanics of reading. Instead, students are expected to read for purposes of understanding and to succeed with sophisticated concepts more or less independently.

An unsuccessful adolescent, therefore, might appreciate a parent who spends some time reading any of the same materials the student is responsible for reading in school. This can help them in dealing with difficult material that they typically may be inexperienced in handling as a young adult, and also show good support of their academic efforts. Just because children know how to read does not mean they know how to read well. Reading with a young teenager can show the teen that a parent is still interested in what they are learning in school, while also providing one more shared experience between them.

In the primary grades, children *learn to read*. This usually includes mastering words (phonics and sight words), as well as beginning to learn to understand what they mean. In the higher grades, children *read to learn*. They no longer need to sound out most words, but are instead expected to understand the concepts they have read.

Today, however, many adolescents graduate from high school without the basic comprehension skills needed to sufficiently understand everyday adult challenges such as the content of written instructions, contracts or agreements. As a result, even colleges and businesses have been forced to add reading classes to their curriculum or training programs to help the large number of functionally illiterate high school graduates.

The Tease of Television

TV has been called chewing gum for the eyes! It is an excellent activity to enable both children and adults to relax from the daily stresses of living. But too much TV, like anything else, can be hazardous. It should be strictly supervised just like other extracurricular activities.

Television privileges don't have to be denied to any child, especially an unsuccessful one who is already coping with enough stress from school. Instead, the *amount* of TV time should be monitored. Consider, for example, that today's average high school student spends approximately four hours per week working on homework and 30 hours per week viewing television! It is easy to see that, if left uncontrolled, such unbalanced time may lead to unsuccessful endeavors, particularly those related to the demanding thinking required of school work.

Teaching Responsibility for Study Skills

Too many parents hold teachers solely accountable for teaching a child the skills of learning responsibility, self-discipline and appropriate work habits—the main ingredients of effective "study skills." If children fail at these study skills, it is presumably the problem and fault of the school. These are not simple skills to teach, nor are they easily addressed by a teacher during a regular school day. The demands on a teacher's time alone often prevent such specialization in curriculum, even when desperately needed.

Some parents rationalize that if they just take care of the physical needs of their child and love them, then they have adequately prepared them to take on most school challenges. In many respects they *will* be prepared, but such elementary needs are obviously not enough to insure school success. Parents should assume the major responsibility for teaching skills *related* to good studying to their child at home, preferably prior to beginning school.

The introduction or mastering of such important skills, therefore, should not be delayed until elementary school is begun. By then, bad habits may have already been established and can be difficult to alter. Lack of appropriate study skills can quickly win a child such negative labels as "unsuccessful" once they are in school, regardless of their good ability to learn.

144

Goal: Hassle-Free Homework

Charlie: Charlie came home from school with the best of intentions for completing his homework before dinner so that he would be free to watch his favorite television shows in the evening. He grabbed an apple and a handful of cookies, plopped down at the kitchen table and proceeded to spread out a stack of rumpled papers.

Shortly after he had settled into his first assignment, his older sister burst through the door with a girlfriend, full of school gossip and giggles. They gathered around Mom in the kitchen and chatted nosily while she prepared dinner.

A little later the phone rang and Charlie's mother sat down at the kitchen table next to him to chat with a longtime friend. After catching up, she glanced at the clock and was surprised to see how long she had talked. Now it was almost dinner time and she felt rushed. "Charlie, quickly clean up your homework and help set the table. It's time for dinner." He obediently shoved his incomplete homework in his backpack, set the table and then grabbed the television guide featuring the evening's programs.

During dinner Charlie's father asked Charlie about his day at school and if he had done his homework yet. "Sure Dad," Charlie replied, "I spent two hours on it. I've been working on it since I got home from school."

"Good job," praised Dad, not knowing that it was neither complete nor done as well as Charlie was capable of. The blame, however, should not be put only on Charlie.

Few school issues cause as much dissention among parents and students than that of homework. Consider some of the more common complaints:

- Parents are unsure of policies surrounding homework.
- Students frequently act confused or appear incapable of handling the assignments independently.

- Parents believe that if they don't monitor homework to see if it is finished and done well, then they aren't doing their job at home.
- Students fear parents' questioning of their capabilities and resent the intrusion of their independent learning.

Obviously, it is easy to see how the battle lines can be drawn quickly even in the most compatible of family relationships when homework becomes such a negative issue.

Defining the Purpose of Homework

It is important to understand what purpose homework has in our children's education before expecting them to be successful with it. Homework can be defined as any type of task accomplished outside of school to help benefit a student's understanding of academic concepts *already taught* in school.

The objective of homework should be to give students independent practice time with skills already mastered in the classroom. Homework should *not* be comprised of learning new, untaught skills. Neither should it be assigned with the expectation of having parents teach their children new skills in the evenings when all are weary from the long day.

Understanding a School's Homework Policy

Much of the confusion over homework can be eliminated by simply finding out the homework policy of your child's teacher, school and school system. Most schools have explicit guidelines outlined for both parents and teachers to follow since homework has always been such a confusing issue between the home and school.

If homework battles are common in your home, understand first that you are not alone. They are indeed common in many households. Disagreements over homework generally begin over a lack of understanding of expectations. To put homework in its proper perspective, your child must first understand the school's homework policy.

Take time at the beginning of each school year (or when the first battle begins) to obtain a copy of the written homework policy from your child's school. If a written policy is not automatically sent home with your child in some form, be sure to inquire about obtaining one, particularly if homework has been a sensitive issue in your home in the past.

Review the homework policy step-by-step *with* your child. It usually spells out clearly the amount of homework assigned at each grade level, as well as specific responsibilities expected of the student. This meeting of the minds, between you and your child, can begin to put the responsibility of homework where it belongs in the first place—on the student, not the parent.

By taking the extra time to understand homework expectations early in the school year, you set the groundwork for eliminating homework battles. You are approaching them from a preventative standpoint instead of one of crisis intervention.

The Responsibility of Homework

Homework is a child's responsibility—not a parent's. Parents have already been to school and accomplished their fair share of homework. Neither is it the responsibility of parents to remind students when to do their homework. Remember, no one reminds parents when to do their work. In other words, becoming responsible for one's own homework can begin to lay the groundwork for other responsibilities in life.

In short, parents should refrain from interfering with a child's homework assignments altogether unless the child asks for help about a *specific* question or problem. A general request for help such as "Will you help me do my homework?" should be refocused as to the particular item needing assistance.

Remember, too, that children who are having trouble getting started frequently have simply failed to read all or even part of the assignment. For example, they may not have read the homework directions well or even read the text material preceding the homework (and on which it is based).

Parents who interfere with children's homework, do not show respect for them. Instead, they show children in subtle ways that they do not believe they are capable of successfully accomplishing independent tasks. Such action implies that they really believe their children to be helpless and useless. These "direct help" measures, no matter how well-intended, are potentially destructive to children's self-esteem and academic confidence, especially when they are trying to understand new skills.

In contrast, if parents want their children to handle homework independently, they should show faith in their abilities and give honest encouragement only when appropriate. Most children rally with such support and perform independently just fine. It is the parent whose own self-confidence is shaky who tends to "worry" that their child may not be doing a good enough job. Consequently, they stand a good chance of crippling their child by very subtly undermining their already fragile self-esteem.

Being responsible for homework requires being a responsible person in other areas as well. Teaching children responsibility means teaching them to "respond" positively to their own good "abilities," even with homework tasks.

Learning responsibility must start long before children begin school. They must experience many successes with being responsible before being expected to succeed with more sophisticated responsibilities, such as homework.

Children naturally learn responsibility in any number of ways—relating to family members, participating in chores and projects and most importantly, observing the way others around them act responsible toward them. Unfortunately, children who do not receive clear signals about the importance of being responsible do not fully understand where their responsibilities lie. This can lead to many problems. In school, homework responsibility problems are a common example.

Tips for Successful Homework

Since parents are not encouraged to supervise or assist their child with homework, what can they do to provide the best possible environment for succeeding with it? Parents can help best in indirect ways by providing, for instance, a quiet place with privacy, a good desk, plenty of school supplies within reach, and appropriate reference materials. These are among the supportive, respectful ways parents encourage good study habits while showing children support and faith in their capabilities.

It is not fair to expect a child to work efficiently at the kitchen table, for example, surrounded by telephones, television, people coming and going or dishes clanging—as "Charlie" was expected to do in his home. Just like adults who work at home, children require a quiet place to collect their thoughts and block out excess stimulation. Otherwise, they will simply not perform at their best in an appropriate period of time.

Parents should regulate, in an unobtrusive manner, the amount of time a child is spending on homework. Is it too much or too little time for the subject and grade level? They should also monitor whether or not they seem to be having a difficult time handling it independently.

In conclusion, if a child begins to experience homework problems, encourage him or her to take the responsibility (there's that word again) to discuss them with the teacher.

Expecting a child to seek help should not be suggested as a punishment or an indication of failure but, instead, an example of how students and teachers naturally work together. They might discuss other ways the child could work to master skills more completely in class before attempting to practice them independently at home again.

Most teachers are very patient and supportive of students approaching them about extra help. Remember, teachers like to teach children—especially ones who are responsible.

The following "homework helper" is an example of a contract designed to help minimize anxiety with children of any age or ability (primarily grades 1-9). I originally created it out of need to aid individual students in untangling their organizational difficulties related to the demands of school. Children who need it appreciate the contract, lean on it heavily and have even been known to share it with their school friends. Something similar may help your unsuccessful child if organizational problems seem to be among the conflicts causing him or her anxiety.

To succeed with the contract, students should try it methodically and consistently for a week or more with a very open mind to insure the greatest success from its use. They should be instructed to review the entire contract prior to beginning homework assignments each day and follow the procedures step-by-step (with help, if necessary) until the routine becomes automatic. Most students who commit themselves to the homework-helper approach begin to see a noticeable improvement with both their homework and learning attitude in as short a time as a week.

Tapping Extra Resources—School Specialists

Parents who deal with unsuccessful children often turn to specialists to help find answers to their children's school-

HOMEWORK HELPER

10 STEPS TO SUCCESSFUL HOMEWORK

NAME: _____   DATE: _____

1 Materials I need for school: (Check)
_ pencils   _ crayons/markers   _notebook   _ pen
_ paper   _ homework notebook _ erasers _ dictionary
_ other _____

2 Homework for tonight: (Check and use the back if necessary)
_____ English/Language Art   ____ Science   _____ Reading

___ Social Studies   ____ Spelling   _____ Math

___ Other (list here):
_____
_____
_____

3 Long-Term Assignments: (Write them everyday until finished)
Subject   Assignment   Day Due   Date Due
_____   _____   _____   _____
_____   _____   _____   _____

4 Check with my homework buddy to make sure I have the correct assignment.
Checked with Buddy?   _____ Yes   ____No

5 List the order in which I will do my homework: (work from hardest to
easiest assignment)   Use the back if necessary.

_____   _____
_____   _____
_____   _____

6 Check off assignment as I finish.   Use a colored pen or marker.

7 After School Today (Today is _____)
Activity   Time of Activity   Time Returned Home

_____   _____   _____

8 List the order I will do everything, including after school activities:
Example: Spelling, Soccer, TV, Math, Dinner, Bath
_____   _____   _____
_____   _____   _____

9 Put all completed homework assignments in a notebook or folder. Put
all materials where they belong (in desk at home, school bag, etc.) Put
all school materials by your door <u>before</u> going to bed.

10 RELAX

151

related problems. Specialists offer a technical approach to difficult educational problems. They consult with parents and teachers alike to help find better solutions to the problems challenging students.

Specialists have training in specific areas such as learning disabilities, speech or language therapy, psychology or counseling, and reading. Although they offer solid help for overcoming school difficulties, they are not miracle workers providing instant cures.

Specialists are regarded as supplementary help for children; their support is not usually in place of regular classroom instruction, but an aid to it. They work with children, individually or in a group, usually during the regular school day.

One of the great strengths of most specialists is their ability to capitalize on the positive, successful side of children, while recognizing their individual needs. They are caring professionals who find challenge in working with exceptional children. Their expertise should not be overlooked when searching for help for any unsuccessful child.

Should I Consider a Tutor?

Private, individual tutors can offer concentrated, one-to-one instruction outside the school to children who need but cannot get enough help in a regular classroom situation to be successful. Tutors best help children manage specific learning challenges that prove too difficult for them to manage in large group situations. Many tutors are highly successful with their students. They are most often able to accomplish more in one hour with a child individually than a classroom teacher is able to accomplish at all because of several factors.

Most importantly, in a tutoring setting, there are few distractions and demands put on the student (as well as the tutor) so they are able to concentrate on specific areas of need.

If your child appreciates individual attention, as most children do, and does not view tutoring as another place to demonstrate his or her inadequacies, then your child might benefit from such an extra resource. Such attention can be expensive, but a good investment in quality time privately spent with a professional. When parents ask their children if they would like some extra help, they are often surprised at their responses. Children who positively respond usually know they are at risk academically and do not want to continue that way.

There are other adults in school settings who can help unsuccessful children in school by showing them special attention in positive ways. These individuals include volunteers (usually parents and grandparents), aides to teachers, peer tutors, or even older unsuccessful children who work effectively with younger unsuccessful children. Older unsuccessful children can learn to see that they (1) are not alone in having a difficult time succeeding with school, and (2) are successful and competent in many other areas, including helping others.

Understanding the Purpose of Grades and Report Cards

Most parents become more than just vaguely interested in their children's learning at the first mention of a report card. Grades have always been extremely important to parents, probably because grades were focused on so much when they too were in school. The fascination and fear of grades carries over to each subsequent generation.

The purpose of grades should be to give students an idea of how they are succeeding with the instructional objectives of each specific school grade. Report cards should reward the achieving student and nudge the underachieving one. They should serve as motivators for learning, not instruments for disciplining or rewarding students.

Unfortunately, schools and teachers too often plot the

standard of measurement for grading students not by an average student in the classroom, but more often by the proficient learner. Sometimes the norms are even set by the highest achieving students in a class because, unconsciously, that is the standard we *want* for all students. It is not only unfair but also adds pressure to already anxious learners—proficient or struggling.

Although not always the case, report cards should provide encouragement for all children, even for those who are not performing well. All children should be able to clearly see skill areas where they excel. Attempts at academic success should also be noted on report cards to encourage children.

Children's interest in their report card and achievement should be at least equal to, if not more than, that of the parents. After all, it is a report of *their* school progress. How should parents best react to their child's report card? Candidly, casually and positively! They should explain to their child what each part means while emphasizing how, because of hard work, their efforts have paid off in specific positive ways.

The same approach should be used with children who receive a less than favorable report card. Parents can best help their struggling student understand negative report card information as a "challenge." Offer honest suggestions for improvement in gentle ways. Like all of us, they are well aware of their own academic shortcomings and usually are overly sensitive to criticism, no matter how well intended.

Many schools now supplement the report card with an interim report. It is an unofficial written report sent out midway in a grading period, which serves as an alert to students in fear of failing a subject. The interim report card is meant to be a positive communication. It alerts students halfway through a grading period that their academic efforts are less than acceptable. It gives them a chance (and expectation) to take better charge of their academic responsibilities.

154

It encourages them to seek ways to succeed with their studies, instead of reacting to failing grades when the regular report card is issued.

Grades should be remembered as being only one measure of a student's competency with a specific skill at a specific time. So much of what children learn well in school cannot be measured by grades, test scores or report cards. Therefore, it is not in a child's best interest to over emphasize grades. Children know the importance of grades; they hear about them daily. They want to look good to their families, their peers, and especially themselves, and they can feel worthless when they don't.

Realistically, grades are not given most of our lives; we do receive rewards and awards (as well as some reprimands and criticisms) for some of our efforts. But most of us labor at learning mainly out of love for knowledge—the intrinsic reward and value. Children, too, must discover the same pleasures of learning instead of accomplishing tasks primarily for good grades.

Bill: Uncle Joe sent Bill one dollar for every "A" he got in school. When Bill was in the lower grades, the dollar bills seemed like millions and he saved them in a cigar box until it was nearly bursting.

In junior high, Bill discovered that the dollars were not really worth millions, and the "A's" had become harder to earn as well. The entire game became pointless to Bill, who has now let the "A's" slip to "C's" and even some "D's" and had long since spent the dollar bills.

But good old Uncle Joe was quick to offer the perfect solution. I'll give you *five* dollars for every "A" you earn now. I bet you'd love that!" Bill was polite, but obviously unimpressed. "Thanks, Uncle Joe, that's okay."

CHAPTER 9

Parents and Teachers Working Together

There certainly is ample information available to help parents and teachers better understand children. It would seem, therefore, that little confusion and misunderstanding should exist between the home and school. Unfortunately instead, the opposite is too often true.

Parents have shown a strong interest in taking the time to help their children succeed at school. A Gallup Poll found that 80 percent of parents who had school-aged children agreed with the idea of attending school themselves one evening a month to learn how to improve their children's behavior and interest in school. This statistic demonstrates that parents are actively interested in their children's school success.

Parents and teachers have so many strengths in common. Both are in direct contact with children on a daily basis, and both have strong feelings about guiding them. Ideally, they work together as one strong ally of children.

Parents and teachers also are children's greatest advocators as well as their audience, tutors and managers for all sorts of school activities. When they effectively work together, parents and teachers have the potential to turn a child's average learning experiences into outstanding ones. For example, teachers recognize that encouragement is their strongest tool for motivating children in any form that works. Similarly, as with Donna's, parents learn from positive school results the importance of using encouragement in home-related activities.

> *Donna:* Donna enjoyed the "contract" her junior high math teacher had designed for encouraging completed homework. He put a check on the contract sheet each day that a student turned in completed assignments. When the student accumulated five consecutive checks, he or she chose a "prize." These prizes included one free night without homework, fun time on the classroom computer, or some goody from the grab bag. Donna worked hard for the incentives and had even begun to enjoy math, now that she was getting better at it.
>
> In a conference, when her mother mentioned that Donna was unmotivated about doing chores at home, her teacher suggested a similar contract approach as a way to encourage Donna to take better care of her dog. Donna's mother agreed to try it. She put a contract (in the shape of a dog) on the refrigerator and a check next to each day Donna fed, watered and walked the dog. After five consecutive checks, Donna chose spaghetti for dinner from the list of "prizes."
>
> At the dinner table that evening, Donna's father remarked how happy everyone seemed—Donna, her mother and even the dog! "What happened? Are we eating some kind of magic spaghetti tonight?" he teased.

Relating Best to Your Child's School

It is essential that parents be as involved as possible with their child's school. They may wish to participate in field trips or other special school events such as parent/teacher conferences and after-school social activities. Through involvement, parents then feel more comfortable and knowledgeable about how today's schools function, as well as better able to understand the areas of education where their child falls short.

Relating well to your child's school also means raising questions about what is being learned in class. Such inquiries reinforce that what goes on at school is important to you at home. It also helps give parents a better perspective of what is really expected in school these days. Surprisingly, many parents go to their child's school and appear shocked at the sophisticated levels of learning he or she is expected to handle. Parents who have not been involved in their child's school frequently have distorted perceptions and misunderstandings about what is really happening inside a typical school.

Teaching Respect for Teachers

Our children's teachers are exceptional people. They most often are hardworking, well-organized individuals who have a keen interest and dedication to working with young people. Teachers have the unique ability to look for every possible potential in a student. They emphasize and capitalize on students' good abilities and small successes while de-emphasizing their disabilities, difficulties and any negative aspects of their learning. Thus, whenever possible, teachers find ways for children to experience even the slightest success.

Teaching children requires tremendous patience, flexibility, toleration and the management of unpredictable human situations. Fortunately, out of necessity, teachers usually possess these traits and abilities.

In addition, most teachers also continue to attend classes themselves (after completing their college degrees) to learn about new methods to challenge their students, because education is in constant change and under public scrutiny. We are forever pursuing the best possible education for our children. If test scores are low, teaching methods are reviewed. When communities are unhappy, school objectives are reevaluated.

Because of such demands, parents have an obligation to teach their children that teachers are professionals who are to be respected. They are capable people whose educational judgment is good. Teachers are the child's advocate, not their enemy. They are dedicated to helping children learn skills that will enhance them throughout their lives.

Labeling School Children

All children react uniquely to each new learning situation. They bring a different set of experiences and expectations to each new challenge. Sometimes, parents and teachers alike find children's uniqueness difficult to understand and are too quick to label them. They pigeonhole children as gifted, quiet, learning disabled or hyperactive, or with other labels that inappropriately describe children early in their educational career, before the children, teachers or parents truly understand their learning styles or labels.

Elizabeth: Elizabeth looked picture perfect each morning when she left for school. Her teacher always complimented her on her neat appearance and pleasant manner.

"Elizabeth is very good," her teacher said to her mother in a conference. "She is never a problem. I am beginning to look closer at her skill level, though. She sometimes has a difficult time completing her work without my assistance or the help of a friend."

"She has always been my good girl," her mother replied. "I never have to worry about Elizabeth in school." But quietly, behind the demure exterior of fancy ribbons and designer jeans, Elizabeth sat afraid in school everyday, afraid that someone would discover that even though she was in second grade, she still had no idea of how to read.

"If I sit very quietly, and smile pretty like I did last year, no one will ever know how dumb I am. They will only see what a good girl I am," she secretly thought to herself. And so, day after day, Elizabeth did just that.

Teacher comments made in reference to children's academic skills and classroom behavior can be insightful to parents. If children show specific learning patterns or behaviors in early grades, for instance, they usually exhibit them at home and throughout their school careers as well, because children tend to act in honest and consistent ways.

Common teacher comments about children such as being friendly, aggressive, argumentative, complacent, shy, extrovertish, a natural follower, a natural leader, etc. can be invaluable for helping parents understand how their children function in school and in a group.

Sometimes parents hear such well-meaning comments about their children and become offended by them. They become unable to focus on any crucial information that might help them arrive at plausible solutions to their children's unsuccessful learning experiences. Successful parents are able to keep an open mind when weighing new information from others about their children and the labels that are attached to them.

The Purpose of Conferencing

Weeks after the new school year is underway—and usually before the second report card arrives home—most schools set aside a block of time for parents and teachers to meet. The parent-teacher conference is a vehicle for meaningful communication between parents and teachers in a relatively short period of time. Constructive information and positive feelings for all is the objective.

Teachers seem to relate to students more personally when they can associate caring family members to them. It seems to add a more human perspective to the "business" of education.

Unfortunately, some parents (and even a few teachers) don't always use their conference time in the most productive ways possible. Previous negative conference experiences going back as far as their own childhood can serve to produce enough anxiety in parents and teachers to cause interference with the positive outcomes that should occur.

Some parents feel thay have little to contribute during conference time. Others do not view themselves in a strong, participatory role in their child's education, instead of realizing that, in fact, they are the cornerstone of it. Parents and teachers can be a strong team when helping to identify and correct most school-related difficulties; neither is totally effective, however, without the other.

Some parents and teachers experience tensions and frustrations from their exchanges. Research tells us that both agree that too much of the communication between them is negative. Perhaps one explanation is that the major communication between the two frequently begins over a negative issue or a crisis situation. Perhaps negative feelings about parent-teacher exchanges linger from past personal experiences. Obviously, such powerful emotions can directly interfere. Sometimes there appears to be a lack of understanding between the two, other times a lack of trust. Where does this leave the child, whose needs prompted the conference?

Children who experience school difficulty normally turn first to their teachers and parents for help. If they discover that the two are unable to effectively work together to find solutions to their school problems, it can produce even more conflict within them. Children may feel they cannot follow a teacher's lead because of differences they have with their parents. They also may worry that their parents' suggestions about managing school are not appropriate.

162

Consequently, struggling children may end up feeling more anxiety over this than that from coping with difficult school tasks! This is the most important time—certainly more than most others—when teachers and parents should pull together to find appropriate solutions to children's problems. Stated differently, the role parents and teachers play in working together for the good of the child (particularly an unsuccessful one) will have powerful effects on them—powerfully negative or powerfully positive. So much is pivotal on the relationship between the parents and teachers.

Jenny: Like most five-year-olds, Jenny was excited when she set off for kindergarten each morning in early September. Her mom drove her up to the front door of the school, gave her a quick kiss and a word or two of encouragement, then drove off. But each day Jenny was late for class.

The teacher talked to Jenny about the importance of being on time and responsible in school. Jenny listened politely and promised her teacher she would try harder to be on time the next day. Jenny's mother continued to drive her to school on time, but each day Jenny was still late.

After two weeks of consistent tardiness, the teacher called Jenny's mother in for a conference. Both were puzzled about the tardiness and both had noticed a sudden change in Jenny's personality. She had begun to act withdrawn and moody and her mother reported that Jenny had begun to complain of stomachaches before leaving for school each morning.

After lengthy brainstorming, they concluded that something unusual must be happening to Jenny between the time she was left at the school door and when she arrived at the classroom door. The next morning after she dropped her off, Jenny's mother discreetly parked her car and watched her daughter. Jenny walked up to the school entrance as usual and struggled to open the very heavy metal door. When it would not open, she struggled more, became frustrated and eventually gave up. Then she sat down by the door and patiently waited for a bigger (and now tardy) student to arrive at school and open the heavy door. Once opened, she quickly slipped inside and ran to class hoping that she was not late again.

An unbelievable story? No, a true one! But because of a productive conference between two who cared—her mother and her teacher—Jenny's problem was quickly resolved early in the school year.

Relating to Your Child's Teacher

Teachers choose their profession because of the great satisfaction and success they find in working with our youth, which is not an easy task. Teachers are hard-working, perfectionistic and goal-oriented. They are honest, sincere people who, like parents, are vulnerable to positive and negative criticism. Teachers are as caring as parents. In fact, most teachers are parents themselves and thus are sensitive about sitting on both "sides" of the desk in conferences.

Teachers who feel secure in their abilities and professional judgment are not easily threatened or frustrated by parents who, when upset, sometimes relate in a combative or abusive manner. For the most part, teachers have their students' best interests in mind even during trying times. No teacher enjoys working with an unsuccessful student. In fact, most view it as a painful, professional failure.

Subjects Warranting a Conference

Parents who are uncertain about when they should confer with a teacher often avoid conferences altogether, letting some potentially serious problems linger too long before apprising teachers of them. Early conferencing can be the best way of avoiding many serious school difficulties. If you have legitimate concerns about your child, teachers appreciate knowing as soon as possible.

Frequently, because of caring parents and sensitive teachers, victories can occur for even minimal problems, like Jenny's in the situation above. For instance, if you feel your child is expected to accomplish too much homework and it seems to be negatively affecting his or her entire life, a short conference may do the trick. Minimal changes can easily be made so that children can experience more success in school and have happier home lives as well.

Similarly, children also can become overly upset by seemingly simple issues such as a seat assignment. By discussing a seat change through a short conference—perhaps with just a phone call—such worries can be quickly eliminated.

Sometimes, very sensitive children will not tell teachers of their school concerns. They feel awkward and embarrassed, and thus it is imperative that parents discuss such concerns on their behalf. Logically, some strategies are best dealt with from the school, while others, especially the emotional side of the child, may be handled more successfully at home.

Occasionally, parents feel that their child's school difficulties are caused by personality conflicts with specific teachers. Nevertheless, there are usually other underlying factors causing conflict that also should be explored. Changing teachers—often the first "quick-fix" suggestion—should be considered as the very last resort in dealing with children's problems. When a child is experiencing anxiety or a lack of success in school, another change—to a new classroom, a new teacher, a new way of doing things, etc.—can only add (at least initially) to his or her frustration and worries. It is also inappropriate for children of any age to perceive that if a situation is difficult to manage, running away from it is the best solution.

Listed below are some appropriate reasons to schedule a parent/teacher conference. It is not meant to be conclusive, but rather to give parents some idea of what is acceptable and expected. Discussions in all parent/teacher conferences should ultimately affect children's school work in positive ways. Both teachers and parents function best when they have the most information to work with. Thus, in a conference it is appropriate to discuss one or more of the items in the accompanying list.

APPROPRIATE TOPICS FOR A PARENT/TEACHER CONFERENCE

1. Levels of instruction
2. Class placement
3. Ability versus achievement of your child
4. Difficulties noted in the child's classes and potential solutions for him or her
5. Grade levels, group levels, etc.
6. Teacher/school expectations at a specific grade or time of year
7. Materials used or needed in classes
8. Academic achievement in relation to peers
9. Health conditions or difficulties
10. Significant family problems or changing family structure
11. Discipline, emotional or physical problems that affect school performance
12. Differences in parental and teacher expectations
13. Negative changes in student attitudes toward school
14. School policy or curriculum
15. *Positive* achievements of your child, even when no difficulties exist.

Scheduling a Successful Conference

Teachers are very busy people. They function around tight schedules and carefully balanced planning. During the school day, they juggle many students' needs and other professional responsibilities simultaneously. Most are quite successful at it, perhaps in part because they tend to have an uncanny knack for organizing chaos.

It is therefore unfair for parents to "drop in" on teachers and expect immediate attention and thoughtful suggestions concerning their children's difficulties. Neither is it appropriate to call a teacher and expect immediate answers for specific problems. Most teachers are caught off guard, although they may not admit it. As a result, their suggestions regarding your concerns may not be the best you could hope for when you catch them "on the run."

In the lower grades, teachers can be held accountable for teaching over 25 students up to a dozen subjects a day. In secondary schools, teachers may have well over 100 students each day. Obviously, when responding to your specific concerns, they need time to reflect on your child's specific difficulties. Children's education can be complicated, and untangling a problem takes thought and time.

The most appropriate way to initiate an effective conference is to first send in a brief note to the teacher requesting a conference. Teachers appreciate thoughtful communication from parents and regard their notes with great importance. Parents can also stop by or call the school office to schedule a conference, if that is more convenient.

In this initial contact, try to express your purpose for conferencing so that the teacher can be well prepared during your time together to address any specific concerns you have.

The Parent's Role in a Conference

Worried parents can gain tremendous relief from an effective parent/teacher conference. Obviously, the quality of the home life for parents as well as children can be greatly enhanced when parents' burdens of school-related problems are lifted. The accompanying list includes suggestions for parents to use in making their parent/teacher conference the most productive.

15 Suggestions for Parents to Assure Positive Conference Results

1. Be respectful of the teacher in making an appointment for a conference. Do not expect positive results from spontaneous conferences over the telephone or in the school hallway.
2. Arrive at the conference promptly at the scheduled time.
3. Be polite and friendly to the teacher; thank them for seeing you and be sincere about it.
4. Prepare in advance by jotting down any concerns or comments you have about your child and their school-related difficulties.
5. Make a list at home of both the positive and negative aspects of your specific concerns, being honest with yourself, your child and the teacher.
6. Go into a conference open-minded, with a positive attitude of working together for the benefit of your child.
7. During the conference, remain focused on the subject; avoid distracting digressions in the conversation. Also, be aware of the time when you are conferencing. Most teachers function on very tight schedules.
8. Respect the teacher as a professional—one who is well educated and experienced—and use his or her good qualities to your child's best advantage.
9. Listen carefully with an open mind and open heart to what the teacher says.

168

10. Be actively involved in the conference, considering all suggestions the teacher makes, as well as making some of your own.
11. Remain calm throughout the conference, in spite of the concerns you are discussing.
12. Summarize strategies that each of you will take to help your child in the best way, at home and at school.
13. End the conference with positive feelings.
14. Plan a follow-up conference at a specific time to discuss the results of any strategies explored.
15. Sincerely thank the teacher for taking the time to consult with you concerning your child's individual problems.

Conferencing With Your Child Present

Including your child in a parent/teacher conference sometimes can be very effective. Primarily, it shows a child firsthand that there are many people around them who care about how he or she is doing in school. Additionally, by including him or her in any discussion, it can help a child focus better on the expectations of an academic program. In expecting children to participate in the conference you also provide them with some feeling of control over their own educational destiny, which hopefully leads to a greater sense of responsibility on their part.

For children who are not being completely honest with themselves, their family or their teachers about school matters, a three-way conference may work especially well. It provides a perfect opportunity for a frank, open discussion among *all* the parties about problems that the child may act vague about at home or at school (either academic or social). The idea of including your child in a three-way conference is a good one. It does however, require more sensitivity and perceptiveness on the parts of the parents and teachers than other conferences if they expect the best results.

Analyzing Children's Test Scores

Another difficult challenge most parents face is that of trying to analyze their children's standardized test scores. Interpreting them can cause even the most rational of parents tremendous anxiety because our society seems to have placed increased emphasis on test scores in recent years. We have seen placement tests, pre-reading tests, and even personality tests targeted for children *younger* than school age! Each test can be scrutinized by several adults and results too often can determine school placement and academic levels. Is it any wonder that so many of our children (and their parents) are already test-anxious by the time they enter school?

Their anxiety seems to only heighten with each advancing grade, eventually leaving some very capable older students almost paralyzed in test-taking situations. Also, it is not unusual for bright children to perform poorly on tests, because they have the capability of seeing a variety of possible answers to questions instead of only one. Obviously, such statistical barriers serve no useful purpose for children later and unfortunately underscore false inadequacies and negative self-perceptions of many very good learners.

Talk to college-bound students about tests. They will tell you that they believe the Scholastic Aptitude Test is the single most important measurement of their abilities. It directly influences not only their college plans and future but also, for too many students, their entire high school experience. More students enroll each year in expensive test preparatory classes, usually on weekends or evenings and with the hope of guaranteeing them even a slightly better SAT score. One has to wonder not only how much knowledge students take away from these experiences but also what lessons in life they learn from the emphasis placed on them.

Currently, there is also controversy over both the cultural biases of such nationwide assessment tests and their relevance to what a child has actually learned. Generally speaking, tests, like grades, cannot *accurately* measure a child's true intelligence or knowledge, and they are, realistically, crude measures of creativity or the likelihood of success in life. At best, they only reflect how well children meet specific demands in taking certain tests at particular times.

Parents can need to step in and help reduce their child's test-taking anxiety by de-emphasizing the importance of the test results. Successful parents keep tests and their results in good perspective. If parents view taking tests as potentially upsetting, they stand to pass on those same negative attitudes to their children.

Retaining Children in a Grade

There has always been considerable controversy over when and why to hold a child back in a particular school grade. Retaining a child in a grade is a serious decision. It sometimes has good results, but it holds no guarantees. People have strong beliefs about retention—parents may feel one way, teachers the opposite, and children can be caught in the middle. If you have ever wrestled with or are presently considering such an issue, perhaps some educational facts and the opinions of educators will help you with such a decision.

Fact: Over a million children are retained in U.S. schools in a typical year.
Opinion: Polled educators presently believe there is a trend towards an increasing number of parents actively pursing retention for their young children.

Fact: Studies on the academic effects of elementary school grade retention have suggested that while many retained students did better by repeating the grade, just as many did worse. Moreover the majority of children studied showed *no* significant difference in academic performance.

Opinion: Polled educators agree that unless a different approach or method is used with children who are retained, most children will show little difference in their academic performance from their previous school year.

Fact: A recent study found that while most children normally made eight to 12 months' academic gain in school, retained children made only six months' gain over the same period.

Opinion: Educators emphasize that grade retention, as with any educational change (gifted, social promotion, etc.), will have lifelong effects on the child, both positive and negative.

Fact: One study found that over 70 percent of high school students who dropped out had failed at least one grade in elementary school.

Opinion: Polled educators agree that the easiest and most beneficial time to consider retention is early in a child's academic life.

Recognizing Symptoms for Retention

Mrs. Teacher: Mrs. Teacher retained two boys in her third grade class last year. A lot of thought, discussion and professional time had gone into the final decision for each child.

It seemed like the best possible option at the time—in fact the only logical one. But now, at midyear, Mrs. Teacher had learned that only one child was finding the retention beneficial. The other child was experiencing more difficulties than the previous year. Everyone, including the children's parents,

172

teachers and principal agreed that both children certainly required more time to learn the basic skills before being expected to proceed to more sophisticated educational challenges.

Given the amount of effort put into each decision, why did one child succeed so easily and the other fail so miserably? And would the situation have occurred if the children had begun their formal education a year later?

Most parents begin considering holding their child back in a grade after observing or hearing about signs of struggle in school. Early in their child's life, many parents see "signs" that clearly indicate their child may need more time—time to mature, build more confidence, understand the world better, develop better peer relationships, or learn to cope better with school challenges. All of these are appropriate signals for considering retention.

Most parents also note "signs" of school stress at home during difficult times. They may observe their child as generally unhappy, listless, withdrawn, "spacey" or disinterested. They may notice an increase in or change of outward behaviors such as fighting, arguing and crying. They may even observe more subtle "signs" such as increased bed-wetting or nightmares, loss of appetite, headaches or stomachaches on school days, or loss of concentration in even fun activities. All of these can be troubling signs. (Refer to Chapter 2 — Warning Signs of an Unsuccessful Child.) It is up to parents and teachers to determine whether or not the trouble is related to academic endeavors.

When Is Retention Appropriate?

Parents and teachers have strong personal feelings about retention; it is a very serious decision.

If a child of at least average intelligence shows good ability to learn well but tends to be somewhat immature, socially or emotionally, retention in an early grade to provide extra time to mature *may* help. Ideally, the child will experience more success for being retained and have more positive feelings about school and him- or herself that will spill over into both peer and family relationships.

Children who are very young in comparison to peers (physically or emotionally) and have specific learning difficulties that can be helped with the aid of special teachers or changes in educational methods, also might benefit from being held back in an early grade.

It is easiest to retain children when they are very young than after many unsuccessful years spent in school and when peer opinion usually matters most to a child. Very young children are also the most adaptable to retention. The problem with considering a young child for retention is that it is far more difficult to access whether a young child is experiencing serious enough trouble to require it. It can be difficult to determine his or her true abilities through standard educational testing procedures because of their tender age. Young children grow and mature differently; they also become aware of their world at different rates.

Young children commonly are retained for lack of maturity. If a child has a late birthday, shows little interest in academic endeavors, or has a difficult time coping with the expectations of the classroom (for example, sitting still, following simple directions or getting along with other children), teachers often discuss retention with parents. Such behavior shows that the child is still very young and need more time just to grow up.

Older students may need to be *considered* for retention only if they are not able to cope with the demands of the school curriculum and are showing any of the signs of stress mentioned earlier.

Considering retention for an older child is a far more serious decision than for a younger one. The older the student is, the more he or she is aware of failure and peer opinion. Those disadvantages of poor feelings about oneself (self-image) and pressures to succeed can far outweigh any of the advantages a child might receive if held back a grade. Also, retention should never be perceived as a punishment for a child who is not finding school a successful experience.

Inappropriate Retention

The type of children who never should be held back in a grade are those whose general intellectual ability lies in the low to low average range. Generally speaking, they will not find much added success by being retained in a grade. They may be already performing at peak levels. To expect more would be unfair. Standard educational diagnostic testing within the school can usually assess children's general intellectual ability to help determine appropriate expectations of them. A change in methods or programs is a more appropriate alternative. Not every child is capable of being the star of the class. Most children are average; a few are above average and a few are below average in significant ways.

Also, it is generally inappropriate to retain children who are physically large (either in height or weight). The potential damage to their fragile self-esteem by being the very largest student in a class of younger children, too may exceed any successful academic progress.

In addition, parents should not consider retention for the purpose of giving their child a year's maturity over other children in the class. Learning doesn't work that way. Children can only learn so much in any given time period, usually determined by their own unique ability and maturity rate, not solely by their size or time spent in any classroom.

Similarly, a child should not be considered for retention with the hopes of achieving exceptional goals sometime in the distant future. Parents sometimes have been known to rationalize that if their young child is retained in school when "it doesn't really matter or when they don't know any difference," he or she may be larger or more agile as compared to their peers. Then the child would stand a better chance of becoming a bigger football star or finer gymnast later in school, for example. Such thinking reflects parents chasing their own dreams through their children. "Slingshotting" children implies holding them back only to spring them forward faster sometime later. Such thinking is potentially as dangerous to children as pushing them ahead a grade or forcing them into accelerated classes when grossly inappropriate.

The Final Decision

When parents and teachers contemplate retention for a child, they should seriously consider all available information—educational, medical and psychological—to help them evaluate keeping the child in a prior grade. Parents, teachers and administrators, together as a team, should spend plenty of unrushed time discussing the child from their own perspectives. Each team member should have an equal voice in the final decision for the child. Specialists, psychologists and medical professionals may be needed to interpret valuable information.

It is important to remember that, in the end, parents—the child's best ally—usually understand what is truly best for their child. Take time to evaluate such a decision. It *will* affect your child forever.

Whatever decisions are made, it is important to understand that they can *always* be reversed or modified. Reevaluation of the retention decision should occur after a short period of adjustment in the new placement, typically between 60 and 90 days.

CHAPTER 10

How Childhood Stress Affects Learning

Most adults envy children's carefree lifestyle. They see them laugh, play and skip off to school each day, thus allowing parents to view their child's world as innocent and insulated from the more complex adult world. But behind the playing and the laughing, children experience many of the same worries in their daily lives that parents do in theirs, and childhood worries lead to the same negative effects of stress those adults commonly experience.

The Problem—Stress, Fear and Anxiety

There are three basic emotional states of being that affect people's behavior—stress, fear and anxiety.

Stress can be a positive emotional state. It can force us to combine our energies to achieve successful ends. Dr. Hans Selye borrowed the term "stress" from the study of physics and applied it to the study of human behavior. Stress, he said, calls for an extra effort on the part of a person to adapt to specific events—good or bad. This extra effort may cause strain or tension on the body, but not necessarily in destructive ways.

Stress can serve as an important motivator for helping people deal with the good events in life as well as the difficult ones. Stress on some level is unavoidable and even necessary if one chooses to function and succeed in life. Nevertheless, as we all know, stress as with other difficult emotions needs to be kept in check so that it doesn't get out of hand, producing such potentially negative results as anxiety.

Fear is a positive and lifesaving as well emotional state. Fear helps us to remain safe by preventing us from doing harm to ourselves or others. It is also the easiest state of being to alter. Remove the fear and the fearful feeling usually goes away. Similar to stress, however, fear must be kept oriented to its healthy aspect, so as not to allow it to become unbalanced and, hence, become converted to anxiety.

Anxiety, in contrast, is a dark emotional state of being. Anxiety is undefined stress and fear all rolled into one difficult emotion. It is one of the strongest emotions we experience and the one that probably causes us the most difficulty in our lives.

Adults are quick to recognize when they feel anxious and attempt to manage those feelings in order to maintain self control. Children, however, are usually not as savvy. They lack an awareness of the sometimes rather subtle symptoms of anxiety, and can be confused by the feelings that lead them to worry. Because they don't recognize and understand the warning signs of anxiety, they are less likely to be able to cope with them satisfactorily. Managing childhood anxiety therefore requires appropriate adult intervention.

Sources of Stress

Anxiety-producing stress is everywhere and affects everyone—the very young, the very old and all ages in between. It is prevalent in not only urban and suburban areas but rural environments as well.

Day to day, people try to cope with stress in order to maintain proper balance in their lives. Necessary changes in one's life, good and bad, can cause stress, labeling even normal life events as "stressful."

The family, in spite of its support and love, can cause its own share of stressful anxiety. Issues of divorce, death, double-income couples, or even the blessing of a new baby in the home can create an environment that has the potential for not just stress but the destructiveness of anxiety.

Causes of Childhood Anxiety

Obviously, there is not one person, group or activity that causes anxiety in children's lives. Instead, there are many factors that contribute and affect them each day.

Everyone and everything seems to contribute—family, friends, teachers, schools and even the children themselves! Parents can demand that a child achieve their high expectations; siblings can rival with each other for parental attention and recognition; and peers can compete for social acceptance, athletic recognition and academic respect. Even teachers (under severe pressure themselves to teach more and faster) can, in turn, innocently transfer their pressure onto their students. Finally, children themselves, feeling pressure from all sides, can become victims by trying to accomplish social and intellectual feats that are very often unrealistic for their abilities, ages or maturity levels.

Not surprising, the media (television, books, newspapers, magazines, movies and records) contribute a fair share of anxiety. Children are exposed to stressful mature issues in an increasingly realistic and graphic manner. Adolescents, who are still quite impressionable, can be hardest hit. Their intellectual capacities and interests are developed sufficiently to be dramatically affected by the media's persuasive viewpoints, yet their emotions and values are still developing and thus remain vulnerable and impressionable.

There are many other reasons children become overly stressed or anxious; these causes can directly affect how they manage school challenges. Fortunately, most situations can be easily managed, however, by caring parents who are alert to their child's needs for help.

First and most importantly, children particularly fear the loss of a parents' love, especially when it relates to their being successful in school. Parents must continually reinforce positive feelings of *unconditional* love by demonstrations that show children they accept them—flaws, poor grades and all.

Second, expressions of shame or criticism about unsuccessful school efforts directed personally at a child can produce such destructive feelings that they cause great anxiety. Parents should always refrain from shaming their children about any school achievement. Shame or criticism can shatter a developing young self-esteem and the good efforts that go with it, and, at the same time, cause unnecessary worry.

Third, friction between parents can create overwhelming anxiety in children and make them feel as if they are in a tug of war. They may fear having to choose sides between their parents as well as the negative outcome of the "war," and their anxious feelings can spill over into their productive school endeavors.

Fourth, anything that interferes with a child's normal developmental routines (including physical activity) has the potential for creating inner anxiety for him or her. Children, like adults, need to learn to work out their daily tensions and frustrations in such natural ways as running, jumping or even just fidgeting. Adults usually work their frustrations out successfully by sitting quietly, exercising or discussing their problems with others. Children, especially unsuccessful ones, need the same advantages.

180

Finally, children may feel anxious when they sense a disrespect of their autonomy (sense of self) and good abilities. All children need many opportunities to learn to function appropriately. For example, they require latitude to decide for themselves what to wear to school, what to buy and whom to invite home, as well as other activities that encourage self-expression, independence and individual decision making.

Childhood anxiety only occurs when children experience stressful or anxious situations (or even perceive an event as such) that causes some physical or emotional reaction. The following are some additional common causes of childhood stress. Reading the list can lead to further insight into the complicated world experienced by children.

- *Pressure to achieve.* Children feel pushed to excel in school, athletics, extracurricular activities and even socially at younger and younger ages.
- *Overloading extra activities.* Although extra activities such as soccer, piano, tennis, ballet and computer classes can be worthwhile for children, their cumulative effect also can be disastrous for them.
- *Violence.* Children, especially young ones, can be confused and upset by the examples of violence they witness on television and movies, or in reading books and magazines.
- *Environmental changes.* Children worry that in their future there might not be enough water, gasoline, money or food left for them.
- *Changing families.* With more divorces and single parent families than ever before, children worry about the future of their own family.
- *Making choices.* Today's children have more choices to make. Poignant social decisions regarding sex, drinking, drugs and smoking are stressful choices for anyone, especially children.

- *Disaster.* Contemplating the possibilities of war and nuclear disaster and its effects can cause great anxiety in young people, especially teens.
- *Latchkey children.* Children who consistently arrive home after school to an empty house and remain alone for long periods of time complain of heightened fears and feelings of loneliness.
- *Birth of a sibling.* Children do not always understand the change in their family position or role brought about by the birth of a sibling. Many fear verbalizing those worries.
- *Death.* Children do not easily understand the abstract concept or process of death. Many experience a great deal of guilt, confusion and anger when faced with those strange new feelings.
- *Moving.* Children lose their sense of connectedness, power, position and friendships when their families move. Many fear the new feelings that typically go along with any move.

SOURCE: Barbara Kuczen, *Childhood Stress*, Delacorte Press, 1982.

Reactions to Anxiety

Often it is not the action or event in a child's life that causes anxiety, but rather the perception or interpretation of it. Children can react anxiously in any number of ways—just like adults. Dealing with their reactions depends not only on their perceptions of the anxiety-provoking event but also their own individual coping mechanisms.

Burnout

Today we hear much talk of "burnout"—student burnout, teacher burnout, job burnout, and even parent burnout. The syndrome has become so widespread in our society that just the word "burnout" has evolved into common household use and conjures up many different messages from humorous to horrific.

In the burnout process, feelings of pressure to perform well increase and become overwhelming. The results usually take the form of discouragement and dissatisfaction on the part of the enthusiastic performer.

Burnout occurs most often to competent individuals who begin their efforts of productivity enthusiastically. Over time, the job, school or home demands become too burdensome. Sometimes failure follows; sometimes the individual develops ailments that are psychosomatic in nature. Too often, dropout (in a job or school) is the end result for competent adults as well as children. Ironically, burnout occurs most often to many of our very brightest and most creative people.

School burnout, like other reactions to negative stress that children experience, cannot be ignored. Instead, its origins must be explored and corrected to significantly alter negative feelings.

Signs of Childhood Worry

It is no secret that today's children are more vulnerable to anxiety in their lives than children of previous generations. The unfortunate fact that they are not any better prepared to cope with it is disconcerting. Often they don't know how to (1) recognize the subtle symptoms of anxiety early enough, and (2) react in appropriate ways that will help reduce or eliminate the stressful situation itself. Instead, most stressful children react inappropriately. Therefore, inappropriately acting children may be children who are secretly suffering form troubling stress.

Some children are unable to express feelings of unidentifiable stress; that is, they cannot, even with help, recognize where their stress is originating. When children feel worried, they often feel inadequate. They can become overly concerned about competition and ambition, and even develop feelings of "over-responsibility."

Children may feel so burdened with anxiety that they act lethargic. These overwhelming feelings of fatigue can cause headaches and stomachaches or other painful symptoms. They also may become self-centered or unstable, lack concentration, suffer moods swings, act withdrawn or appear apathetic.

Anxious children frequently can act absentminded, be "spacey," and lack focus. Some become isolated from those to whom they should be closest, most often their families. Their worries outside of school can easily transfer to inside school and vice versa, thus affecting their good ability to succeed anywhere. Fortunately, most teachers sense when children have something stressful on their minds, because most often their behavior dramatically changes.

All children have strong feelings of anxiety at some time, but children who consistently exhibit a number of the signs of anxiety over a prolonged period of time should be suspected of harboring serious anxiety-related difficulties that could interfere with their school success.

Adolescents are special children who at their rapidly-maturing age, need special consideration. Many adolescents frequently misunderstand themselves and their new emotions. They desire protection from the world like children but total independence like adults.

Anxious adolescents are really fragile "large children." They can have exaggerated feelings of fear, anger or guilt as well as insecurities about their own competence—socially or academically.

Signs of Anxiety

The following list further elaborates more specific signs of physical and emotional reactions to anxiety. It is not an all-inclusive list but does serve as a guide for identifying the warning signs.

How Childhood Stress Affects Learning

SIGNS OF ANXIETY

Bed-wetting
Boasts of superiority
Complaints of feeling afraid or
  upset without being able to
  identify the source
Complaints of neck or back pains
Complaints of pounding heart
Complaints of stomach upset,
  queasiness or vomiting
Compulsive cleanliness
Compulsive ear tugging, hair
  pulling, or eyebrow plucking
Cruel behavior toward people or
  pets
Decline in school achievement
Defiance
Demand for constant perfection
Depression
Dirtying pants
Dislike of school
Downgrading of self
Easily startled by unexpected
  sounds
Explosive crying
Extreme nervousness
Extreme worry
Frequent daydreaming and retreats
  from reality
Frequent urination or diarrhea
Headaches
Hyperactivity or excessive tension
  or alertness.

Increased number of minor spills,
  falls and other accidents
Irritability
Listlessness or lack of enthusiasm
Loss of interest in activities
  usually approached with vigor
Lying
Nightmares or night terror
Nervous laughter
Nervous ticks, twitches, or muscle
  spasms
Obvious attention-seeking
Overeating
Poor concentration
Poor eating
Poor sleep
Psychosomatic illness
Stealing
Stuttering
Teeth grinding (sometimes during
  sleep)
Thumb-sucking
Uncontrollable urge to run and
  hide
Unusual difficulty in getting along
  with friends
Unusual jealousy of close friends
  and siblings
Unusual sexual behavior such as
  spying or exhibitionism
Unusual shyness
Use of alcohol, drugs or cigarettes
Withdrawal from usual social
  activities

SOURCE: Barbara Kuczen, *Childhood Stress*, Delacorte Press, 1982, p. 14.

Managing Childhood Anxiety

Anxiety negatively impacts our sense of order and balance. Since it is unrealistic to think that we can avoid all stress in our lives, it is essential that we learn to use it in productive ways to prevent the more damaging stress—anxiety.

Teaching children how to cope with anxiety is an asset to them; it can reassure them of feeling in good control of their lives. It is parents' responsibility to teach them *how* to best manage their anxiety. Parents are the perfect teachers to do so because most have experienced plenty of anxiety in their own lives and also understand their children better than anyone else. However, in order for parents to effectively teach their children about anxiety, they must first learn to deal with their own anxieties in effective ways—not always the easiest challenge for any of us.

Society has encouraged us to teach our children to function more like miniature adults at younger and younger ages. Today's children look older in their "designer" clothes, engage in more sophisticated activities and also cope with more stress.

Curiously, our society on the other hand doesn't encourage our children to cope with stress in ways that we adults typically turn to (medicines, alcohol, drugs, therapy, exercise, etc.). Thus, our children have had to learn to relieve their stress and anxiety in their own ways, although often not the best ways. Suicide, for example, now is the third leading cause of teenage deaths. Teen pregnancies occur in extraordinary numbers. Violence in the home and school is on the rise, and thousands of our children are "missing." Are these reactions the best ways our children have learned to cope?

Joey: Joey, a fourth grader, had a standing appointment every Tuesday afternoon to talk to a psychologist. Usually they talked about school. Sometimes when they talked, Joey cried; other times he stuttered or made up false stories about how he

186

was doing in school. Recently, he had stopped talking altogether and had become noticeably withdrawn.

This particular Tuesday, Joey pulled his latest report card out of his pocket and handed the crumpled paper to Dr. Smith through tearful eyes. Expecting "D's" or worse, Dr. Smith looked over the solid "B" report card. He asked Joey why he seemed upset since the grades were obviously good.

"My brother got all A's," Joey mumbled as he looked down. However, no matter how Dr. Smith explained his feelings about school, grades or even his brother, Joey left the doctor's office feeling pretty dumb and worthless.

Why is Joey so anxious about school and grades at such a young age? How will he feel about the future if the stress of the present is already too great for him to bear? And most importantly, how will Joey manage any increasing stress?

Children begin to learn to deal with anxiety in small amounts when they are very young. Small mistakes can teach important lessons. But if parents are too overprotective and quick to jump to the aid of their frustrated or confused child, they eliminate opportunities for their child to identify and begin to learn about coping with stress and anxiety.

We mothers can be the worst offenders. Our role, as one said, is to overprotect the children; while the role of the father is to protect the children from the overprotection of the mother!

If children learn to handle minimal amounts of anxiety successfully while they are very young, they most likely will have the ability to handle anxiety more effectively throughout their entire lives.

Coping With Anxiety—An Individual Decision

The most effective way for children to learn to manage anxiety is to identify it as specifically and as early as possible.

187

As with other subjects of concern, it is far easier to deal with anxiety in more preventative ways then reactive ways.

Each child learns to cope with anxiety in his or her own personal way. Understanding and respecting children's unique personality helps parents teach them to manage anxieties in effective ways. After all, compensation of difficulties is the best weapon there is against feelings of inferiority. Such a positive attitude also reassures children that they really are in good control of their own lives, no matter how anxious.

Anxiety-Free Homework

For school children, pressure for excellence (often mislabeled as encouragement) from the home and school creates added anxiety. Unfortunately, many students can become so paralyzed by the pressures created from the many demands that they end up hopelessly unable to perform at all! One of the greatest daily school pressures students attempt to manage is the completion of homework. Some are successful with it, but just as many students are not.

One suggestion to help insure the successful completion of homework—and thereby relieve the anxiety that frequently encompasses it—is to introduce a homework contract. The discussion of homework in Chapter 8 contains a "Homework Helper" contract that can be used to relieve the anxiety associated with homework.

Contracts can be viewed as organized crutches or stress relievers, but if they help students cope better with their lives, then they can be tremendously worthwhile, particularly for short time periods. Children who are responsible for challenging academics frequently have extracurricular commitments with demands exceeding their regular school commitments. They may need help juggling such complex lifestyles if they are to succeed with any of them.

Warning: The Cycle of Anxiety

Today's "super-parents" are quick to encourage their children through any activities that will make them more "special" children, even when it means tight schedules at inappropriate times. "Good" parents sacrifice because they believe that they are providing "the best" for their children.

They admit that even though they provide the money, transportation, time or support for the special activities, they are stressed by the mayhem of doing them. What parents don't easily acknowledge though is that their children, too, are just as stressed by these activities. If parents don't take the time or initiative to teach their children how to deal with the troublesome anxieties these extra activities often cause, the level of anxiety only increases for children, in spite of the devotion to the activities themselves. As in the diagram on the next page, the vicious cycle of anxiety continues.

Managing Anxiety

In today's world, learning to manage anxiety may mean discovering the pleasures of relaxing, for both parents and children. For children (particularly anxious ones), relaxation means aimless play. But because so many of our children have such rigidly planned lives, there is little time or encouragement to relax. Casual play allows children natural opportunities for unwinding in their own individual way, thus preventing, build up of anxiety in their young, complicated lives.

Children who appear to be caught in the middle between anxiety and demands, need opportunities to reassess their lives, usually requiring either cutting back on the pressures or increasing the supports so that they may be able to better cope. Adjustments must be made at the onset of the signs of anxiety because continuing in the same manner will not help children in any way but could add even more anxiety.

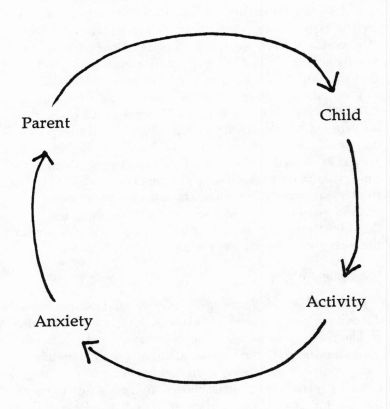

THE CYCLE OF ANXIETY

CHAPTER 11

Proven Steps to "Making the Grade"

When struggling children finally begin to find success in school, parents and teachers notice dramatic positive changes. Soon the changes become apparent to others, which helps to contribute to children's improved attitude towards school. Parents and teachers get tremendous satisfaction in watching unsuccessful children blossom and see themselves as the productive individuals capable of accomplishing great things that they always were. It is like watching magic keys open stubborn doors.

This final chapter is a compilation of practical ideas from teachers, specialists and even parents for helping unsuccessful children turn all their learning experiences into positive results. Although the list is not meant to be all inclusive, it does contain many suggestions that if followed offer real hope and encouragement.

Parents and children may gain insight from reading this chapter, together or individually. The ideas have been categorized by those best managed by the family and the home, the school, and the world outside the home or school. These suggestions—or steps to making the grade—are not listed in any preferential order and, of course, not all of them need to be followed to achieve positive gains in helping your individual child. Finally, following the list of suggestions is the positive conclusion to Emily's difficulties, which you read about in Chapter 1.

Steps Related to the Family and the Home Environment

- *Believe in yourself*, your parenting abilities, and the child you know best.
- *Love your child unconditionally*. Avoid putting stipulations on your love such as showing your love for your child only as a reaction to their stress or accomplishments. Let your children know they are *loved for themselves*, not for what they do or how well they perform.
- *Openly show affection* to your child. It helps them better understand and "feel" your love and respect.
- Show your child, by example, that having *fun is an important part of life*. Leave the worries of teaching to the school and its professionals.
- *Encourage your child to relax*. Children need time every day to unwind and be carefree. It helps rejuvenate them.
- Encourage a *balance of work, play and relaxation*. This emphasizes purpose in life and also helps to relieve anxiety.
- Set good, *positive examples* for your child. Let them see through daily example how successful you have been in finding genuine happiness in life.
- Pay more attention to the *simple day-to-day activities* of living and less attention to material objects and achievements.
- *Be communicative with your child in loving ways* through eye contact, talking, touching and actively engaging in activ-

ities with them. Effective communication is confidence-building for both children and parents.

- *Encourage open communication*, especially about homework or troublesome school-related tasks. Try to ask only nonjudgmental questions about your child's efforts.
- Praise your *child's attempts at acting in mature ways* when they try. Ignore less than successful efforts as much as possible.
- *Encourage independence* and independent thinking. Praise your child's independent efforts and acts, and refrain from doing for your children what you know they can do for themselves.
- *Instill curiosity* in your child. It will serve them lifelong. Curiosity helps children find satisfaction in themselves and their world. Worried feelings interfere with natural curiosity.
- Make a *clear statement of the expectations* you have of your child. Make them simple and direct so they cannot be misinterpreted.
- Provide opportunities for your children to make their *own decisions* and allow them to see the natural consequences of them, even when they occasionally arrive at inappropriate ones. Decision-making reinforces confidence and independence.
- Take time to *answer your child's questions*, even when they appear frivolous. This, too, encourages curiosity and helps make the bond between parent and child stronger.
- *Never underestimate your child's ability* to do things for themselves. It helps them understand independence and self worth. Avoid hovering over your children, waiting for them to fail, which can translate into feelings of ineptness on their part.
- Set aside time to *train your child* to perform those life skills that will insure them success in many ways. For example,

if they need instruction in how to clean their room so they can find their things or work and play more comfortably, take time to show them how. Don't take even the simplest of skills for granted. All skills must be learned and reinforced often to become successful.

- *Praise any good values* your child demonstrates. If your teenager has a party, for instance, and puts the house back in good order afterwards, praise them for doing a good cleanup and for respecting the home as a place of order for all. Refrain from criticizing how messy it was.
- *Show respect* for your children by treating them respectfully. Talk to them as any other valued person. Ask their permission before retelling a story about them or showing something of theirs to others. Asking permission lets them know you respect them and their feelings. They, in turn, will learn to respect you and themselves more.
- *Show good faith* in your children. It helps them believe in themselves and gives them courage to try new things.
- *Eliminate criticism* and replace it with encouragement.
- Remember that *praise is valuable only when honest.* It should not be given constantly or haphazardly. Praise should focus only on children's efforts and accomplishments, *not* their character or personality.
- *Evaluate* your children in *positive terms.* It protects their ego and gives them the courage to take new risks.
- Let your child know that he or she is *not expected to be a superstar*—academically, athletically or socially.
- Avoid encouraging *perfectionism.* Perfectionism is not required in everything we do in life in order to achieve happiness and success.
- Refrain from telling children how "good" or "smart" they are. It places too much pressure on them. Be aware of well-meaning comments like "it doesn't matter what grades you get or what job you choose, as long as you do

your very best." Even this can put too much pressure on a child. Being the "best" can be perceived as an impossible goal, especially for any unsuccessful child.

- *Avoid teaching too much* at home. It, too, adds pressure to children. Leave the academic teaching mainly to the teachers. Children want their parents to be parents, not their school teachers.

- Be a *good listener* to your children. Hear their needs, fears or frustrations. Learn to help them express their anxieties by verbalizing their feelings for them. "You seem sad this morning," for example, sets the stage for more open communication and also helps children get in better touch with their own feelings.

- Let your children know that *how they feel* inside is important to you as well as them. Reassure them that their feelings, both positive and negative, are acceptable to think about and talk out.

- *Ignore misbehavior* as much as possible. Praise positive behavior instead.

- *Withdraw from conflict* with your child whenever possible and instead, enlist your child's cooperation in handling difficult situations. It helps him or her feel needed and better understand the purpose of rules.

- Use *rewards* cautiously. When a child is struggling and experiences some small success, rewards often can serve as "crumbs of encouragement" to keep trying. Big rewards are not necessary, and they need not be material. Verbal praise—the reward most effectively used by educators—is appropriate for most efforts. Fancy gifts or extravagant time spent on activities for small accomplishments serve little meaningful purpose.

- Place *less emphasis on punishment*. Instead, increase verbal communication about respect for self and others, self-worth, and the uniqueness of each individual.

- *Avoid punishing a child at home for doing poorly in school*; it

195

is not appropriate. There may be many reasons a child does not succeed in school. Any academic efforts deserve some praise. Punishment related to school can be defeating as well as create feelings of wrongdoing and inadequacy in children. Accept the challenge of demonstrating how loving and supportive you are to your child, especially during difficult times.

- Give your child the *most precious gift—your time*. If the quantity of time must be limited between you and the children, be responsible about the quality of time you spend with them. Let them know that the best rewards in your relationship are not with money and objects, but time spent together in meaningful ways.
- Provide a variety of *stimulating experiences* for your child. He or she learns something new from each experience and each helps foster a stronger bond between parent and child.
- Create an *orderly environment* in your home. Consider how the structure and routines in your home help your child cope with the structure and order he or she must manage successfully at school.
- Help your children *learn to organize their life* so that its functionality aids them in all their efforts. Encourage mental activities to help them learn to better organize their thinking, and also provide opportunities for them to learn to organize their physical lives.
- *Give your child meaningful responsibilities*. Household chores, getting up on time, etc. help children learn to feel comfortable with the responsibilities they consistently face in a school environment.
- *Provide a variety of books and magazines* in your home to enrich your child's environment. If students do not experience books as vital in their lives, chances are they will not view book learning as important either.
- See that your child has all the necessary *materials at home*

196

to accomplish schoolwork efficiently, chiefly a desk, pencils, paper, dictionaries, reference books, quiet space and especially uninterrupted time.

- *Praise all contributions* that your children make to the family, themselves, school and society. It reinforces that he or she is worthwhile and fits appropriately in this world, Unsuccessful children can feel painfully disconnected with the world around them.
- *Monitor your child's health* (including nutrition, exercise and adequate rest) to provide the best physical advantages possible. No one functions well when not feeling healthy and alert, and children are certainly no exception.

Steps Related to School

- *Appreciate any efforts* your children's teachers put forth on their behalf.
- Let your children know that you realize *school can be difficult.* Remind them that you, too, were once a student who also found learning difficult at times. Reassure them that their concerns are legitimate and that you truly understand. Be available to listen at times when you are unrushed and have an open mind.
- *Avoid overstating how important school is,* because children already know it is important. Instead, emphasize how learning something new is exciting and satisfying.
- *De-emphasize grades.* Alternately, emphasize the joy of learning. Many children (and parents) can become obsessed about getting good grades.
- *Be sympathetic* when your children don't do well in school. Let them know you understand new skills are difficult to learn. Be there not only to listen but to help them verbalize their feelings or fears.
- *Avoid acting angry* when a child is not succeeding.

197

- Let your children know that it is sometimes *acceptable to get less than perfect results in academics*. Few of us can consistently maintain a 100 percent effort without sometimes letting down.
- Help your child understand the *purpose of studying*. Curiously, many children don't realize why they should study. Teach them that learning new skills is satisfying and makes us happier because we are better able to understand and appreciate our world.
- *Encourage good study skills.* Teach your children that learning good study skills may be difficult at first, but improves each year, banking on the previous year's successful experiences. Eventually, study skills become easier, more effective and automatic. There is hope when trying to learn them.
- Emphasize to your child that *learning good note-taking skills* requires excellent listening and organizational skills as well as good writing skills. Those students who learn how to take notes effectively have a far greater advantage over those students who do not learn how well.
- Teach your child *how to take notes* if he or she does not already know. Note-taking skills are frequently overlooked in school curricula because of lack of time. It is a skill that even good students do poorly.
- Encourage *learning good research skills* by beginning to teach them to children as early as pre-kindergarten. Help them learn while young by such examples as beginning to classify vegetables in the refrigerator, fruits in the fruit bowl, or things in the living room that begin with a "B" sound. Such skills help young children begin to think in organized ways, even prior to attending school. Be available to support complex research skills with older students. Many competent students become easily frustrated and give up.
- *Employ a variety of questioning techniques* with your child in daily interactions. In school, children are expected to

succeed with different types of questions—factual and open-ended, as well as high-level, critical-thinking questions.

- *Establish a regular time of study* each day for your children, particularly if they seem unsuccessful and inundated with schoolwork. Such structure guides them more easily into productive work.
- *Avoid becoming involved in your child's homework* unless he or she asks for specific help. Homework belongs to the child and, indirectly, the school—not the parents.
- *Avoid forcing* your child to complete homework assignments or school projects immediately after arriving home from school or at the very end of a long day. Those are transition times when children generally need personal time to unwind and relax.
- Recognize that most *homework complaints* come more from the child disciplining themselves to do the tasks than from being overwhelmed by the academic demands of the assignments.

Steps Related to the World Outside School or Home

- *Limit the number of extracurricular activities* your children are engaged in. Let them become focused and competent with only one or two activities. It can help them feel special and happy about something fun. Too many extracurricular commitments turn life into a series of flashing moments, instead of a flow of treasured memories. "Too much, too soon" also leads to early burnout. Consider delaying participation in formal activities until your children are very receptive and overly curious about them. Never talk them into activities.
- Encourage only *non-threatening competition.* It helps build confidence in children. Unhealthy and unnecessary competition puts too much stress on children's fragile self-esteem.

- Avoid expecting *perfectionism or high performance from extracurricular activities*. It, too, can create too much pressure on the child. Instead, emphasize the fun of the activity, and be listening and ready to react positively when the child no longer wishes to pursue it. Too many meaningless activities spread children too thin and does not allow them enough time to relax, unwind, and spend quality time with the family at home.

When the above suggestions are applied to real problems of real children, real miracles often occur. Unsuccessful children are not hopeless. They can be helped, and problems can be eliminated when parents are willing to invest the time and patience it can take. But what else do any of us have that we would rather invest in if not our own children?

Consider, for example, the important difference the efforts of Emily's mom, her teacher, and Emily herself made in turning her school problems around.

Emily: [Continued from Chapter 1]
Emily's problems, unfortunately, had to grow worse before they began to get better. Emily received failing grades in school subjects she knew very well, and the teacher began to talk about retaining her in the same grade the next year. Emily seemed smart enough, but it was impossible to give her good grades if she didn't do the work.

By spring, the seriousness of Emily's school problems prompted a formal conference between Emily's mother, the teacher and the principal. It focused on one last joint effort to save Emily from retention. They agreed on a rather rigid but functional approach to Emily's problems.

At home, Emily's mother sat down with her and discussed restructuring their home life to help Emily study better. First, they worked together to reorganize Emily's room. They separated the clothes from the clutter and set up a quiet place in her room just for studying. They bought a cute lamp for the previously unused desk, as well as a bookshelf for school books and reference materials. All toys were removed from the desk drawers and replaced with school supplies. Then Emily and her mother worked together on the rules for study time.

Television time was well-defined as was playtime and bedtime. One chart was designed and displayed on the refrigerator for monitoring chores; another was taped to the back of the front door listing what to take to school each day. Emily also had a homework contract in a notebook to help her keep her school assignments well organized.

At school, Emily's seat was moved closer to a responsible friend and also within easy reach of the teacher. The teacher occasionally called on Emily to repeat directions to the rest of the class for helpful reinforcement. Her work load was significantly reduced until she found more success and then was gradually increased without her realizing it.

Next, Emily was given pleasant responsibilities at school to help her feel good about herself. She was line leader, lunch money monitor, etc. She ran notes to the office where the principal seemed somehow to always be present to ask Emily how she was doing in class.

Her teacher gave her honest praise whenever possible, and even arranged for Emily to work with a school specialist on the more difficult academic challenges.

Things began to turn around for Emily, gradually at first, and then more rapidly after she experienced some success. She began to feel well-connected to her class and even invited a new friend home after school a couple of times.

Time at home began to shape up more pleasantly as well. Emily seemed more relaxed. She related better to her family and was cheery and helpful.

Shortly after she began to find success, Emily arrived home with her report card. There was a marked improvement in all areas, especially attitude. Emily ran up her driveway waving the usually dreaded report card. "Look Mom, I got a good report card. I did great. I think I did better because I like school now. When I'm all grown up, I want to still be in school. There's so much to do there that's fun. Maybe I'll even become a teacher!"

Bibliography for Recommended Reading

Books

Albert, Linda. *Coping with Kids and School*, New York: Ballantine, 1984.

Ames, Louise Bates, Clyde Gillespie and John W. Streff. *Stop School Failure*, New York: Harper and Row, 1972.

Berger, Eugenia Hepworth. *Parents as Partners in Education*, St. Louis: The C.V. Mosby Co., 1981.

Bloom, Benjamin and Karen Zelan. *Developing Talent in Young People*, New York: Ballantine, 1985.

Briggs, Dorothy Corkille. *Your Child's Self Esteem*, New York: Dophin, 1975.

Brazelton, T. Berry. *Toddlers and Parents*, New York: Dell, 1974.

Chess, Stella and James Whitehead. *How to Help Your Child Get the Most Out of School*, New York: Doubleday, 1974.

Dinkmeyer, Don and Gary D. McKay. *Parent's Handbook: Systematic Training for Effective Parenting*, Circle Pines, MN: American Guidance Service, 1976.

Dinkmeyer, Don and Gary D. McKay. *Raising a Responsible Child*, New York: Simon and Schuster, 1973.

Dobson, James. *Dare to Discipline*, Wheaton, IL: Tyndale House Publishers, Inc., 1970.

Dreikurs, Rudolf. *Children the Challenge*, New York: Hawthorn, 1964.

Elkind, David. *The Hurried Child*, Reading, MA: Addison-Wesley, 1982.

Elkind, David. *Miseducation: Preschoolers at Risk*, New York: Alfred Knopf, 1987.

Fontenelle, Don. *Understanding and Measuring Creative Children*, New Jersey: Prentice-Hall, 1983.

Freudenberger, Herbert J. and Geraldine Richelson. *Burn Out*, New York: Bantam, 1981.

Ginott, Hiam. *Between Parent and Child*, New York: Avon, 1965.

Goldberg, Herman and Gilbert Schiffman. *Dyslexia*, New York: Stratton, 1972.

Gordon, Thomas. *Parent Effectiveness Training*, New York: Peter Wyden, Inc., 1970.

Greene, Lawrence J. *Kids Who Underachieve*, New York: Simon and Schuster, 1986.

Johnson, Eric. *How to Live Through Junior High School*, New York: Lippincott, 1975.

Johnson, Spencer. *The One Minute Mother*, New York: William Morrow and Co., 1983.

Kappleman, Murray and Paul Ackerman. *Between Parent and School*, New York: Dial Books, 1977.

Kuczen, Barbara. *Childhood Stress*, New York: Delacorte, 1982.

Lightfoot, Sara Lawrence. *Worlds Apart*, New York: Basic Books, 1978.

Miller, Mary Susan. *Bringing Learning Home*, New York: Harper and Row, 1981.

Moore, Raymond and Dorothy Moore. *Better Late Than Early*, New York: Simon and Schuster, 1971.

Pearce, Joseph. *The Magical Child*, New York: Bantam, 1977.

Piaget, Jean. *The Language and Thought of the Child*, New York: Meridian, 1959.

Silberman, C.E. *Crisis in the Classroom*, New York: Random House, 1970.

Simon, Sydney, Leland Howe and Howard Kirschbaum. *Values Clarification: A Handbook of Practical Strategies for Teachers and Students*, New York: Hart, 1972.

Trelease, James. *The Read-Aloud Handbook*, New York: Viking Penguin, 1979.

White, Burton L. *The First Three Years of Life*, New York: Avon, 1975.

White-Bowden, Susan. *Everything to Live For*, New York: Pocket Books, 1985.

Bibliography for Recommended Reading

Ziglar, Zig. *Raising Positive Kids in a Negative World*, Nashville: Thomas Nelson Publishers, 1985.

Zimbardo, Philip. *The Shy Child*, New York: Doubleday, 1982.

Articles

Bettleheim, Bruno. "Why Children Don't Like to Read," *Atlantic Monthly*, Nov. 1981, pp. 11–38.

Moles, Oliver C. "Synthesis of Recent Research on Parent Participation in Children's Education," *Educational Leadership*, Vol. 40, No. 2, Nov., 1982, p. 44.

Merriman, Vivian. "A Word to Parents," *Pennsylvania Counselor*, January, 1983.

National Education Association Booklet. Reprinted from *Today's Education*, April, 1971.

Seginier, Rachel. "Parent's Educational Expectations and Children's Academic Achievement: A Literature Review," *Merrill Palmer Quarterly*, Vol. 29, No. 1., January, 1983.

Vernon, Libby. "Who Is Responsible for Our Children's Education?" *Childhood Education*, Vol. 60, No. 4, March/April, 1984, pp. 274–5.

Walberg, Herbert J. "Families as Partners in Educational Productivity," *Phi Delta Kappan*, Vol. 65, No. 6, February, 1984, pp. 397–400.

Weinstein, Claire and others. "How to Help Your Child Succeed in School," National Institute of Education, U.S. Department of Education, Washington, D.C., March, 1983.

Zigli, Barbara. "How to Help Your Child Make the Grade," and "Ninth-Grade Cure: More Learning and Less Teaching," *USA Today*, January 28, 1985, p. 3D.

Index